THE TAKING OF BERLIN . . .

Fifty minutes to zero hour. An ominous, tense silence, disturbed only by the crackling of burning buildings, hung over the city. Suddenly we heard a child crying. It seemed to come from somewhere underground. Muffled yet insistent, the child's voice kept repeating *"Mutter, mutter,"* a word all of us knew.

"Seems to be on the opposite bank," said Sergeant Masalov.

Machine guns began to stutter. Sergeant Masalov crawled forward, pressing himself to the ground, taking cover in shallow shell craters. He was careful to feel every bump and crack in the asphalt so as not to hit a mine. He got across the embankment and hid behind a projection of the concrete canal wall.

Masalov leaped over the parapet. A few more minutes passed. Enemy machine guns stopped firing for a moment. Holding their breath, our men waited for the child to cry out again. But no sound came. They waited five minutes, then ten more. Some of the men began to get ready to charge. Then they heard Masalov's voice: "Attention! I have the child! Cover me! A machine gun on the right, on the balcony of the building with columns. Shut 'em up!"

But it was already time for the artillery preparation. General Pozharsky who commanded the army's artillery gave the order: "Ready. . . . Fire!"

Thousands of guns and mortars opened up on the enemy defenses, covering Masalov's withdrawal from the jaws of death. . . .

BATTLES HITLER LOST

AND THE SOVIET MARSHALLS WHO WON THEM

MARSHALLS ZHUKOV, KONEV, MALINOVSKY, ROKOSSOVSKY, ROTMISTROV, CHUIKOV, AND OTHER COMMANDERS

JOVE BOOKS, NEW YORK

The publishers are grateful to the
Novosti Publishing House for their cooperation
in furnishing material for this book.

This Jove book contains the complete
text of the original hardcover edition.
It has been completely reset in a typeface
designed for easy reading, and was printed
from new film.

BATTLES HITLER LOST

A Jove Book / published by arrangement with
Richardson & Steirman, Inc.

PRINTING HISTORY
Richardson & Steirman edition published 1986
Jove edition / July 1988

ISBN: 0-515-09643-1

Jove Books are published by The Berkley Publishing Group,
200 Madison Avenue, New York, New York 10016.
The name ''JOVE'' and the ''J'' logo
are trademarks belonging to Jove Publications, Inc.

PRINTED IN THE UNITED STATES OF AMERICA

10   9   8   7   6   5   4   3   2   1

Contents

Foreword

BY MARSHAL SERGEI SOKOLOV*

Dear American readers,

This is a book about the battles of the Second World War, which were unprecedented in scale and ferocity. In these battles, the Soviet people fought against Nazi Germany and its satellites and won a world historic victory, together with other countries of the anti-Hitler coalition. This is not a chronological account of the war, but a book of reminiscences by Marshals of the Soviet Union Georgi Zhukov, Ivan Konev, Konstantin Rokossovsky, and other military leaders who commanded our troops during major large-scale operations.

*Marshal of the Soviet Union Sergei Sokolov (b. 1911) has served in the Soviet Army since 1932 and is a graduate of the Armored Forces Academy and the Academy of the General Staff.

During the Second World War, Marshal Sokolov was Chief of Staff of the commander of the armored and mechanized troops of the Karelian Front and commanded an army's armored and mechanized troops. After the war, he commanded a tank regiment and a division, and later was commander of an army, Chief of Staff of a military district, and then commander of a military district. In 1967 he was appointed First Deputy of the Minister of Defense, and on December 22, 1984, he was given the post of Minister of Defense of the USSR.

The years slip by, and the hard times of the war are receding further and further into the past. But people the world over—those who themselves lived through the horrors of war and those who were born and have grown up under a peaceful sky—turn to that period of history again and again. It is important from today's point of view to understand the lessons of the past so that we can resolve the paramount issue of the present: how to preserve peace and life itself on earth.

Sixty-one countries—more than 80 percent of the entire population of the world—were plunged into the crucible of the Second World War unleashed by Nazi Germany. Its flames engulfed the territory of 40 countries and spread to seas and oceans. From September 1939 to May 1941, the Nazis captured many countries in Europe. They trampled underfoot the soil of Poland, Denmark, Norway, Belgium, Holland, Luxembourg, France, Greece, and Yugoslavia. The blitzkrieg, which had led to the enslavement of almost the whole of Europe, persuaded the Nazi leaders of the Reich that they were unconquerable. It convinced them that they could fulfill their hopes for world domination. But they had the Soviet Union to deal with on their way to that end.

To attack the Soviet Union, the Nazi coalition had put together an enormous force: 190 divisions, more than 4,000 tanks, about 5,000 planes, and over 47,000 guns and mortars. As day was breaking on Sunday, June 22, 1941, the immensity of that huge force—treacherously and without a declaration of war—crashed down upon our country, which was engaged in peaceful work. The Nazi invaders used the most barbarous and inhuman methods of a total war of devastation against the Soviet people.

As soon as the Soviet Union entered the war, the peoples of Europe and the entire world looked toward it with hope, considering it a real force capable of defeating Nazism. Being well aware that the fate of their own countries depended largely on the outcome of the fighting on the

Soviet-German front, the governments of the United States and Britain decided to enter into an alliance with the Soviet Union in the struggle against the common enemy. Winston Churchill, the Prime Minister of Great Britain, declared at the end of June 22, 1941 that "the Russian danger is . . . our danger, and the danger of the United States" and that, therefore, Britain would give whatever help it could to Russia and the Russian people. On June 24, Franklin Roosevelt, the President of the United States, also stated his readiness to help the Soviet Union in the war against Nazi Germany.

Nazi Germany and its satellites were defeated by the joint efforts of many countries. The peoples and armies of the United States, Britain, and other countries of the anti-Hitler coalition made a great contribution to victory. A courageous struggle against the Nazi invaders was waged by the military contingents and partisan armies and detachments of Yugoslavia, Poland, and Czechoslovakia. It was fought by the patriots of Bulgaria, Romania, Albania, and Hungary, and by the members of the Resistance and the anti-Nazi underground.

The Soviet Union, however, bore the brunt of the struggle against the Nazi bloc. In an extremely difficult and serious situation, the Communist Party and the Soviet government were able to mobilize all the materiel and human resources of our multinational country for the Great Patriotic War against the treacherous enemy. They turned the country into one military camp. In his reminiscences, Marshal Georgi Zhukov talks about the early period of the war when, thanks to the heroic efforts of the Soviet people and their armed forces, it had become clear that Hitler's military venture was doomed to failure.

Marshal Vasili Sokolovsky recalls the Battle of Moscow at the end of 1941 in which the Nazi aggressor suffered the first major defeat since the beginning of the Second World War. In this battle, the Soviet Army frustrated Hitler's blitzkrieg plan and destroyed the myth of the Wehrmacht's "invincibility."

Of vital importance in bringing about a decisive change in the Great Patriotic War and in the Second World War as a whole was the Battle of Stalingrad, during which hand-picked German divisions were encircled and destroyed and a large number of troops were taken prisoner. In his reminiscences, Marshal Andrei Yeremenko reflects on how the brilliant victory at Stalingrad enabled the Soviet Supreme Military Command to take the strategic initiative firmly into its own hands.

The Nazi leadership's desperate attempt to recapture this initiative during the Battle of Kursk in the summer of 1943 ended in another crushing defeat for its armies. Nazi Germany was now on the brink of catastrophe. The Battle of Kursk is described by Chief Marshal of the armored forces, Pavel Rotmistrov.

The reminiscences of other Soviet military leaders are devoted to the events of 1944. Soviet troops had liberated the entire country from the Nazi invaders and set out on their victorious offensive to the west, driving the enemy out of many European countries.

This was the military-strategic situation in Europe by the time the second front was opened in the summer of 1944. But even then the Soviet armed forces continued to be the main force in the anti-Hitler coalition. In 1945 they inflicted fresh and powerful blows upon the enemy. The war ended with the great Berlin operation and the unconditional surrender of Nazi Germany.

Soon afterward, in fulfillment of its allied commitments, the Soviet governments declared war on militarist Japan with the intention of eliminating the remaining seat of the world war in the Far East, ensuring the security of Soviet borders, and bringing about an early peace. Marshal Alexander Vasilevsky describes the crushing defeat which the Soviet armed forces inflicted upon Japan's one-million-strong Kwantung Army.

The victory secured by the Soviet people and their armies was perfectly natural. They fought a just war of liberation, defending the freedom and independence of their country, the world's first country of socialism. Fighting the Nazi invaders, the Soviet armed forces were also defending world civilization and the right of all peoples to determine their own destiny.

The figures cited below testify to the decisive role the Soviet Union played in smashing the Nazi war machine. During the 1,418 days of the war, the Soviet armed forces smashed and captured 507 German divisions and 100 divisions belonging to Germany's satellites, whereas the Allies defeated 176 enemy divisions in Western Europe, Northern Africa, and Italy. The Wehrmacht lost over 75 percent of its aircraft, nearly 75 percent of its tanks and assault guns, and 74 percent of its artillery on the Soviet-German front. Winston Churchill wrote that "there was no force in the world . . . that would have been able to maul and break the German army unless it had been subjected to the terrible slaughter and manhandling that has befallen it through the strength of the Russian Soviet armies."

It was also a convincing victory for the Soviet socialist economy. Despite the temporary occupation of many industrial regions by the enemy, as a result of which many Soviet plants and factories had to be moved to bases in the east, during the war Soviet industry turned out nearly twice as much military equipment as Nazi Germany.

The lend-lease deliveries of military hardware from the United States helped the Soviet people to some extent in their struggle against the Nazi aggressor, but these deliveries did not play a decisive role. President Roosevelt, for one, did not believe that the lend-lease agreement was a major factor in defeating Germany. He said as much, adding that the Soviet Union primarily used arms produced by its own factories.

Regrettably, there are people who are engaged in an unworthy attempt to prove that the defeat of the German army in the war against the Soviet Union was accidental. They seek to belittle the Soviet Union's role in winning the victory and to play down the importance of the Soviet leadership's strategic guidance and the skill of Soviet troops. I hope that the reminiscences of Soviet military leaders to be found in this book will help you to gain a proper understanding of this question.

The Soviet people's victory in the Great Patriotic War is a lesson of undiminishing significance, evidence of the strength and invincibility of the socialist state. Those who attempted to destroy our country's integrity and independence and our system have been thrown onto the rubbish heap of history. But the Soviet Union is thriving, developing, and forging ahead.

The Second World War, the most bloody and devastating in history, is a thing of the past. We must not forget, however, that its terrible wounds had not yet been completely healed at a time when the clouds began to thicken once more. People around the world were being frightened by a falsehood about a "Soviet military threat." The Soviet Union's enemies began to ascribe aggressive intentions to a country whose efforts and aspirations were being wholly concentrated on restoring a war-ravaged economy and on peaceful construction. These absurd inventions were a smoke screen for the establishment of military blocs spearheaded against the Soviet Union and the other socialist countries, for the construction of military bases close to the Soviet Union's borders, and for unleashing an arms race unprecedented in scale and fraught with sinister consequences.

The entire history of the Soviet Union testifies to its firm devotion to a policy of peace and international friendship, a policy of struggle against war. The Soviet government has unilaterally pledged itself not to be the first to use nuclear weapons, and it has called on other nuclear powers to follow suit. It has put forward a large number of constructive proposals, including those for an immediate freeze on nuclear arsenals and for a general and complete ban on nuclear-weapons tests. The Soviet Union is not seeking unilateral advantages over the United States and other NATO countries; neither does it intend to gain military superiority over them. But it will not allow any other country or coalition of countries to achieve superiority. The Soviet Union is consistently striving to put a stop to the arms race and prevent the militarization of outer space. Its ultimate goal is to have all nuclear weapons in the world destroyed and to eliminate the threat of nuclear war once and for all.

Today, when mankind is threatened with nuclear danger, it becomes imperative to learn the main lesson of the last war: war must be opposed before it has broken out. In the hard times of the Second World War, the Soviet Union and the United States were able to pool their efforts in the struggle against their common enemy. In the 1970s they were able to cooperate fruitfully for the sake of curbing the arms race and improving the international situation. Cooperation between our two countries is also vital today, over forty years after the great victory. However tense and complicated today's international situation, there still exist genuine opportunities for preserving peace and strengthening international security. These opportunities must not be missed.

I would like to conclude by wishing the readers of this book and all the American people peace and prosperity.

Marshal of the Soviet Union
Sergei L. Sokolov

Minister of Defense
of the Soviet Union

The Soviet Union in the Second World War

MAP No. 1

At dawn on June 22, 1941, Nazi Germany attacked the Soviet Union. After a powerful artillery preparation and air strikes the German troops invaded the Soviet territory along the entire Soviet-German border. Hitler and his generals sought not only to conquer the Soviet people but also to eliminate the socialist state of workers and peasants, kill as many Soviet people as possible and settle the conquered territories with German colonists. The Great Patriotic War of the Soviet people against Nazi Germany began. It lasted 1,418 days and nights.

Making use of the surprise attack and the superiority in forces, especially in tanks and aircraft, the Wehrmacht received a temporary advantage. Germany hurled east 190 divisions—5.5 million men, 47,000 guns and mortars, 4,300 tanks, and about 5,000 planes.

The Soviet Army opposing these forces had 2.7 million men, 37,000 guns and mortars, 1,500 tanks, and 1,600 planes.

The German divisions were fully manned and equipped and had a two-year experience of waging war. The Soviet troops were armed with outdated weapons and their supply of ammunition was inadequate. Most of them were far away from the border, engaged in peacetime training exercises.

In the main directions of their thrusts the Nazis' superiority was fourfold. The Soviet defense comprised pockets of resistance. German tank units bypassed them and struck from the rear and against the flanks. Soviet Army units were forced to fight in encirclement or retreat east.

Despite heavy losses, the Soviet troops were engaged in active defensive fighting. A handful of defenders of the Fortress of Brest held out for a month. Odessa and Kiev fought back for over two months. The Battle of Smolensk lasted two months, and in it the Germans were temporarily forced on the defensive—for the first time in the Second World War. By the middle of July 1941 the Wehrmacht had lost one half of its tanks and about 1,300 planes. By the end of September about 535,000 German soldiers had been killed. The German Command's blitzkrieg plan was failing and the war was assuming a protracted character. The Soviet industry was being restructured in the rear and put on a war footing, and fresh reserve divisions were being formed. A guerrilla movement began on enemy-occupied territory.

The formation of the anti-Hitler coalition was speeded up after Nazi Germany's attack on the Soviet Union. The leaders of Great Britain and the United States declared their support for the Soviet people. Their representatives came to Moscow to attend a conference on October 29–November 1, 1941, at which a plan was adopted for deliveries to the USSR of armaments, foodstuffs, and industrial plant. From the Soviet Union strategic raw materials were to be delivered to the U.S. and Britain. It was a first step toward the Allies' joint action against Nazi Germany and its satellites.

MAP No. 2

By late September 1941 the German troops had sustained tremendous losses and were stopped at Leningrad, Vyazma, Kharkov, and on the approaches to the Crimea. The Nazi Command decided to throw its main forces for the capture of Moscow. Hitler thought this would enable him to decide the outcome of the war at one blow. To implement this plan the German generals assigned 1.7 million men, 1,700 tanks, about 1,400 aircraft, and 14,000 guns and mortars.

The Soviet Command also regarded the Moscow sector as the decisive one and concentrated there 40 percent of its troops engaged on the Soviet-German front. A state of siege was declared in Moscow. Half a million of its residents were building defense fortifications on the near and far approaches to the city. Tens of thousands of Muscovites joined volunteer detachments. Fresh units and materiel arrived from near areas. General of the Army Zhukov was appointed commander of the forces defending Moscow.

The Battle of Moscow began in late September and lasted for two months. The German Command twice attempted "all-out assaults." It threw into action dozens of crack divisions. In some sectors their advance units came as close as 25 km to Moscow. But the Soviet Army stood firm. Meanwhile the Soviet General Headquarters secretly concentrated reserve divisions from Siberia for delivering counterblows.

By the beginning of December the German offensive had spent itself. Choosing the right moment, the Soviet Army went over to the counteroffensive. On the very first day of the battle, on December 5, the Soviet regiments broke through the enemy's lines in several sectors. Giving the enemy no chance to regain control, they drove him westward. By late March 1942, the Soviet Army had thrown back the German troops 150 to 400 km away from

Moscow. Huge territories in central Russia had been freed
from the enemy. The Wehrmacht had lost over 500,000
men killed. A great amount of German materiel lay abandoned on the battlefields.

It was Nazi Germany's first major defeat in the Second
World War. The Soviet victory at Moscow contributed to
the intensification of the liberation struggle in the European countries occupied by Germany. An anti-Hitler coalition was formed in the summer of 1942. The USSR, the
U.S., and Britain signed agreements on alliance in the war
against their common enemy—Nazi Germany.

MAP No. 3

In late July 1942 the Wehrmacht began a second general
offensive on the eastern front. The German Command,
which did not have sufficient forces for active operations
in all the strategic sectors, directed its main efforts southward. Later on the Nazis planned to advance toward Moscow and eastward. Concentrating one-fifth of their infantry
and one-third of Panzer formations in the south, the Germans broke through the Soviet defensive lines north of the
Sea of Azov and pushed toward Stalingrad. At the same
time they pressed their offensive in the Kuban River area
and in the North Caucasus.

The Soviet Army, which was on the defensive, had
fewer forces and less materiel than the enemy. After fierce
fighting the German units managed to break into Stalingrad
and reach the Volga. The situation had become critical. In
mid-September the Nazis captured Mamayev Hill dominat-
ing the city. Fresh forces were rushed to the aid of the
defenders. They recaptured the hill at heavy costs. The
fighting was especially intense in the area of the railway
station, which changed hands several times. The Soviet
soldiers were fighting for every block and for every house.
The "Pavlov house," which became legendary, was at-

tacked by the Germans many times. But the handful of its defenders, led by Sergeant Pavlov, repulsed all their attacks.

When the battle was at its height the Soviet Command concentrated large reserves on the flanks of the German grouping. Fresh infantry and tank divisions and many artillery units had been brought up. The Soviet counter-offensive began on November 19 from two directions. Soon 22 Wehrmacht divisions and many other units, totaling 330,000 officers and men, were encircled.

All the attempts by the Nazis to relieve the encircled troops were foiled. By early February 1943 the resistance of the German units was broken. The remaining troops surrendered. Field Marshal Paulus and 24 generals were taken prisoner.

In the course of the Battle of Stalingrad, which lasted 200 days, the Nazis lost 1.5 million men, over 3,000 tanks, 4,500 aircraft, and 12,000 guns and mortars.

The Soviet Army's victory at Stalingrad was a turning point in the entire Second World War. It shook the Nazi war machine to its foundations. Resistance was gaining scope everywhere on the territories occupied by the Nazis.

MAP No. 4

In early September 1941 the German troops broke through to Lake Ladoga and completely encircled Leningrad with its 2.5 million residents. The front line ran several kilometers from the city, which was continuously bombed and shelled. The Nazis decided to starve the population and the defending troops. Lack of food in the city was compounded by a harsh winter. There was no fuel or electricity, the city's transport did not run, and the water supply system had failed. The bread ration was cut down to 250 grams a day for workers and 125 grams for children and office employees. There were virtually no other food rations. Soldiers received only a little more food than workers.

But neither the savage artillery bombardment and air raids, nor famine could break the fighting spirit of the Leningraders. Workers did not leave their plants for weeks on end in order to give the troops more weapons and ammunition. Scientists and cultural workers did much to preserve things of artistic and scientific value. The city could be reached only by a route across Lake Ladoga when it became icebound. That route came to be called "the road of life." Hundreds of thousands of children and women were evacuated, and ammunition and food were supplied to Leningrad along this road.

The siege of Leningrad lasted for more than a year. All the attempts by the Soviet troops to break through the blockade were unsuccessful. Finally, the victory at Stalingrad made it possible to provide conditions for breaking down the blockade of Leningrad. The enemy, who had concentrated all his reserves at Stalingrad, could not reinforce his troops near Leningrad in the event of a Soviet offensive.

In the morning of January 12, 1943, after a powerful artillery preparation, the divisions of the Leningrad Front dealt a strong blow in the eastward direction against the enemy positions near Lake Ladoga. A fire storm raged for two hours over the enemy fortifications. Then the infantry rushed into the attack. To meet it a strike army of the Volkhov Front was making headway. After fierce fighting going on for a whole week the Soviet troops liberated the town of Schlisselburg as well as other populated localities that had been turned into centers of resistance. The troops of the two fronts pierced the blockade and linked up. A railway was laid along a corridor 8 to 10 km wide. It was along that railway that Leningrad was supplied with food, fuel, weapons, and ammunition.

One year later, in January 1944, a decisive battle at Leningrad began. The Soviet Army broke down the enemy's defenses and completely lifted the blockade. Leningrad had lived under a blockade for 900 days and nights. About 700,000 of its inhabitants had died from hunger and cold. The defense of the city went down in history as an example of the staunchness and mass-scale heroism of the Soviet people.

MAP No. 5

In the course of the battles in the North Caucasus in the summer and autumn of 1942 the Soviet troops were forced to leave the Taman Peninsula, and the port of Novorossiisk. The Nazi army needed this port badly to bring in supplies. But the Soviet troops which had entrenched themselves nearby on the eastern bank of the Tsemess Bay prevented the enemy from using the post. The Nazis made frequent attempts to drive the Soviet units away from the coast but failed.

After the Nazi debacle at Stalingrad the Soviet Command decided to liberate the Taman Peninsula. The blow could be delivered only in the area of Novorossiisk, for in other places it was more difficult to break through the enemy defenses because of the marshy terrain. Much hope was placed on the surprise effect and audacity of the attack.

A head-on offensive on Novorossiisk failed, however, for the enemy's defenses proved to be too strong. So sea- and airborne troops were landed in the enemy's rear in late January 1943. The main landing force west of Novorossiisk found themselves under a heavy enemy fire and could not get a foothold. But the auxiliary force that was landed south of the port on February 4 managed to gain and consolidate its foothold. Soon over 2,000 marines were dug in on the beachhead. The enemy made repeated attacks to drive them off into the sea, but the Soviet troops did not abandon their positions, and reinforcements kept coming. The Soviet soldiers called the beachhead "Little Land."

Throughout the spring and summer the Germans kept

the beachhead under artillery and machine-gun fire. In the daytime it was continuously bombed by aircraft. German ships intercepted and sank transports that were bringing reinforcements, weapons, and food for the marines. But the latter stood firm and beat off all enemy attacks. For 225 days the Soviet soldiers fought on that tiny piece of land, pinning down up to five enemy divisions.

In the autumn of 1943 the Soviet forces stormed Novorossiisk again. On September 10, after a powerful artillery raid on the city, the regiments of the 18th Army advanced from the north and east. Landing parties broke into the port in torpedo boats and captured the railway station. Assault-landing troops attacked from the Little Land in the south in a converging blow. After fierce battles the Nazi forces were dismembered and began retreating hastily westward across the Taman Peninsula.

The breakthrough of the German defenses at Novorossiisk made the situation for the Wehrmacht troops in the Kuban area more difficult. In early October the Taman Peninsula was completely liberated from the Germans.

MAP No. 6

The defeats in the 1942–1943 winter campaign, especially at Stalingrad, weakened Nazi Germany. In trying to reverse the course of events at any cost, Hitler and his aides carried out total mobilization, gathered all the reserves, and threw them to the eastern front. Up to two-thirds of all the Wehrmacht's forces were concentrated there.

In the summer of 1943 the German Command decided to carry out Operation Citadel, whose purpose was to encircle and destroy a large grouping of Soviet forces in the center of the Great Russian Plain, at the cities of Kursk and Orel, and then to launch a new offensive on Moscow from the south.

Soviet intelligence saw through the enemy's intentions in time. Necessary measures were taken—the troops built powerful fortifications and a superiority in manpower and materiel was achieved. A grouping consisting of 1.3 million men, 20,000 guns and mortars, and 3,400 tanks and self-propelled mounts was facing a German force comprising 900,000 officers and men, 10,000 guns and mortars, and 2,700 tanks.

The exact day and hour of the German offensive—3:00 A.M. on July 5—became known from prisoners' evidence. Three hours before the offensive Soviet artillery opened fire. The German troops brought forward for attack sustained heavy losses, but the whole machine of the offensive had already been set into motion. Weakened Nazi divisions advanced with a delay.

Fierce fighting broke out. At the cost of tremendous losses German units in some sectors drove wedges into the Soviet defenses to a depth of 10 to 15 km. On July 12 a tank battle, the biggest in the Second World War, took place at the railway station of Prokhorovka, 30 km north of Belgorod. Altogether 1,200 tanks and self-propelled guns took part in it. In the engagement the German units lost 400 tanks and over 10,000 men. The following day the Nazis assumed the defensive everywhere.

The Soviet troops inflicted a series of powerful blows on the enemy and passed over to the offensive. On August 23 Kharkov, a major industrial center, was liberated. The Wehrmacht lost over 500,000 men, 1,500 tanks, 3,000 guns, and 3,500 planes at Kursk.

After their defeat at Kursk the German forces never recovered. They were thrown back beyond the Dnieper by consecutive blows from different directions. The initiative passed to the Soviet Command. From that time on it was the Soviet Army that chose the time and place of major strategic battles.

MAP No. 7

Fierce fighting was raging on the banks of the Dnieper
throughout October 1943. The Soviet divisions tried to
consolidate and widen the bridgehead they had seized on
the right bank, while the Germans attempted to dislodge
them. To build up the German strength the Wehrmacht
transferred from Western Europe about ten combat-ready
divisions. Battered units were moved from the east to
replace them after a rest and reinforcement.

General Vatutin, who commanded the Soviet troops,
prepared an operation to rout the enemy's Kiev grouping,
as a result of which Kiev, capital of the Ukraine, would be
liberated. Soviet regiments went over to the offensive
twice. The main blow was struck from the south, from the
Bukrin bridgehead, and an auxiliary blow—from the Lyutezh
bridgehead, north of Kiev. But the enemy's strong defenses could not be broken through.

Then the Soviet troops were regrouped. At night, tens of
thousands of men and hundreds of tanks were secretly
moved at Veliky Bukrin from the right bank of the Dnieper
to the left bank. They marched 200 km to the north and
again crossed the river to the right bank at Lyutezh. The
weather was rainy. On the one hand, this was fortunate:
German aircraft could not carry out reconnaissance, but on
the other, the rains had made the roads impassable and
even a small fire could not be kindled to dry up. It was in
such conditions that a tank army and two infantry corps
were transferred from the southern bridgehead to the northern one in nine days. Only wooden dummies of tanks and
guns had been left in the old places to mislead the enemy.

On November 1 the Soviet troops struck the first blow
from the Bukrin bridgehead, but it was a feint attack. The
Nazis thought that the Russians' main forces were still
there and committed all of their reserves. Then an unexpected and powerful blow was struck from the north, from

the Lyutezh bridgehead. The enemy began retreating hastily, leaving behind weapons and wounded. The front line was broken through. On the night of November 5 fighting broke out on the outskirts of Kiev, gradually shifting toward the center of the city. A brigade of Czechoslovak volunteers distinguished themselves in street fighting. It was commanded by Colonel Ludvik Svoboda, future President of Czechoslovakia. By the morning the storming ended. The capital of the Ukraine, which had for over two years been languishing under the yoke of the German occupation, was liberated.

Bringing in fresh forces, the German Command began a counteroffensive on November 15, trying to throw the Soviet forces back beyond the Dnieper, but the enemy's offensive was stemmed. Thus a huge bridgehead was formed on the right bank of the Dnieper—up to 500 km long and 200 km deep. Soon afterward new attacks by the Soviet Army were launched from it, sweeping the Ukrainian lands west of the Dnieper.

MAP No. 8

In order to break the enemy's back the Soviet Command struck a series of surprise blows in 1944. First they were dealt in the north, then in the south, again in the north, and then in the center of the Soviet-German front that extended over 2,000 km. Here and there whole enemy groupings surrendered after they were encircled.

On January 24, the units of the Second Ukrainian Front launched an offensive in the south of the Ukraine. German positions formed an outward salient as a result of the advance of Soviet forces near the city of Kirovograd. A blow was delivered at the base of this salient from the south. The following day a strike grouping of the First Ukrainian Front delivered a blow aimed at linking up with the other advancing Soviet troops.

The forces of the two fronts struck converging blows and linked up in the area of Korsun-Shevchenkovsky. The enemy's ten infantry divisions and one motorized brigade found themselves bottled up, and the ring of encirclement was tightening. The offensive was effected despite the absence of good roads. Horses and even cows were used to bring in ammunition, fuel, and provisions. Local residents helped carry artillery shells and cartridges.

The German Command was frantically looking for ways of rescuing the encircled grouping. It removed large forces from other sectors of the front—eight Panzer and six infantry divisions. But all their attempts to break the ring of encirclement were futile.

The showdown came in mid-February. The Soviet Command proposed humane terms for the surrender of the encircled German troops, but its proposal was rejected. Thereupon Soviet bombers went into action and the artillery and mortars opened fire. The end result was a rout of the German grouping: 55,000 German officers and men were killed, and 18,000 were taken prisoner. Huge quantities of German weapons and equipment were abandoned.

The front line was pushed back far to the south of the Ukraine.

MAP No. 9

The Nazi leaders wondered where the Russians would begin their next major offensive in the summer of 1944. They thought it would be launched in the north of the Ukraine, and concentrated there over 100 divisions.

But the Soviet Command decided to carry out an operation for the liberation of Byelorussia. It was given the codename of Bagration, after an outstanding Russian general, hero of the 1812 war against Napoleon. Four fronts were to take part in the operation: First Baltic, First Byelorussian,

Second Byelorussian, and Third Byelorussian fronts, supported by Byelorussian guerrilla detachments.

The forces of the four fronts comprised 1.4 million men, 31,000 guns and mortars, 5,200 tanks and self-propelled guns, and over 5,000 planes. The Soviet troops were considerably superior to the enemy both in manpower and in materiel.

On June 23 a cyclone of artillery fire descended on the enemy. To cramp the Nazis' maneuvering, guerrillas began simultaneously to blast bridges and tracks on many railways. German logistics become disorganized. The forces of three fronts began the offensive at the same time, and the following day one more front joined the battle. This was unexpected to the Nazis, and their defense soon collapsed. As early as June 24, the forces of the First Baltic Front assault-crossed the Western Dvina and emerged in the rear of a large enemy grouping. The troops of the Third Byelorussian Front were advancing to meet up with them. When they linked up, five enemy divisions had become encircled near Vitebsk. At the same time the forces of the Second Byelorussian Front were pressing the offensive toward Mogilev, while the units of the First Byelorussian Front were advancing through the southern areas of Byelorussia. A major enemy grouping was encircled and destroyed at Bobruisk. On July 3 Soviet troops broke into the capital of Byelorussia, Minsk, closing the ring of encirclement. Over 100,000 enemy soldiers were caught in a giant trap. The main forces of the Wehrmacht's Army Group Center were routed.

The Soviet Army's advance westward continued with increasing momentum. In late July its advance units reached the Baltic coast. After a strong enemy counterblow, however, they were forced to retreat. The troops of the Third Byelorussian Front encircled the German garrison in Vilnius, capital of Lithuania. After five days of fighting the city was captured. Pursuing the enemy, the units of the First

The War Begins

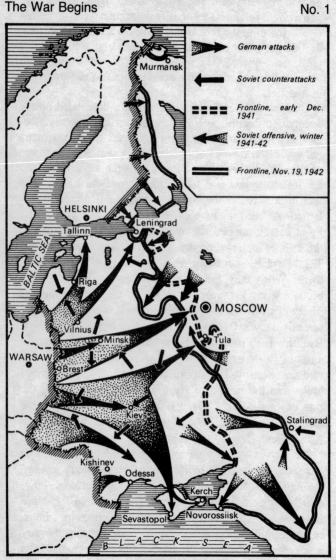

The Battle of Moscow

No. 2

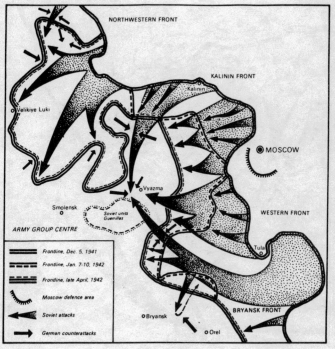

NORTHWESTERN FRONT

KALININ FRONT

Kalinin

Velikiye Luki

MOSCOW

Smolensk

Vyazma

Soviet units
Guerillas

WESTERN FRONT

ARMY GROUP CENTRE

Tula

	Frontline, Dec. 5, 1941
	Frontline, Jan. 7-10, 1942
	Frontline, late April, 1942
	Moscow defence area
	Soviet attacks
	German counterattacks

Bryansk

BRYANSK FRONT

Orel

The Battle of Stalingrad   No. 3

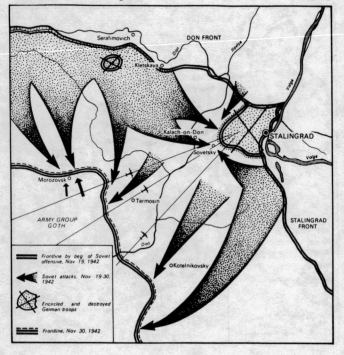

DON FRONT

Serafimovich

Kletskaya

Kalach-on-Don

Sovetsky

STALINGRAD

Morozovsk

Termosin

ARMY GROUP
GOTH

Don

Kotelnikovsky

STALINGRAD
FRONT

Frontline by beg. of Soviet
offensive, Nov. 19, 1942

Soviet attacks, Nov. 19-30,
1942

Encircled   and   destroyed
German troops

Frontline, Nov. 30, 1942

Breaking the Siege of Leningrad   No. 4

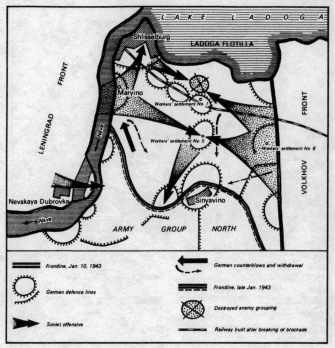

Novorossiisk   No. 5

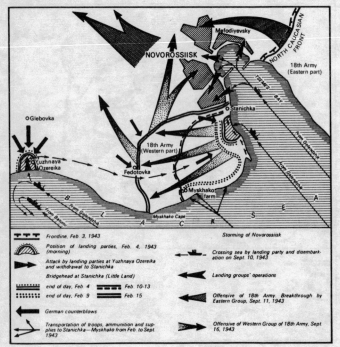

Myskhako Cape

Frontline, Feb. 3, 1943

Position of landing parties, Feb. 4, 1943 (morning)

Attack by landing parties at Yuzhnaya Ozereika and withdrawal to Stanichka

Bridgehead at Stanichka (Little Land)

end of day, Feb 4   Feb. 10-13

end of day, Feb 9   Feb. 15

German counterblows

Transportation of troops, ammunition and supplies to Stanichka—Myskhako from Feb. to Sept. 1943

Storming of Novorossiisk

Crossing sea by landing party and disembarkation on Sept. 10, 1943

Landing groups' operations

Offensive of 18th Army. Breakthrough by Eastern Group, Sept. 11, 1943

Offensive of Western Group of 18th Army, Sept. 16, 1943

The Tank Battle at Kursk

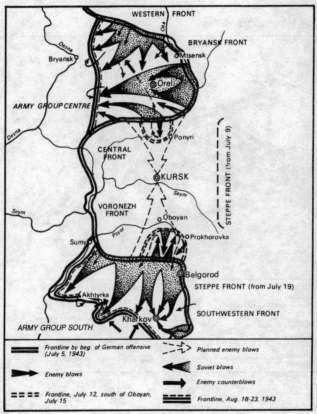

WESTERN FRONT

BRYANSK FRONT

Oka

Desna

Bryansk

Mtsensk

Orel

ARMY GROUP CENTRE

Desna

Ponyri

CENTRAL FRONT

STEPPE FRONT (from July 9)

KURSK

Seym

VORONEZH FRONT

Oboyan

Seym

Psyol

Sumy

Prokhorovka

Belgorod

STEPPE FRONT (from July 19)

Akhtyrka

Kharkov

SOUTHWESTERN FRONT

ARMY GROUP SOUTH

Frontline by beg. of German offensive (July 5, 1943)	Planned enemy blows
Enemy blows	Soviet blows
Frontline, July 12, south of Oboyan, July 15	Enemy counterblows
	Frontline, Aug 18-23, 1943

The Liberation of Kiev   No. 7

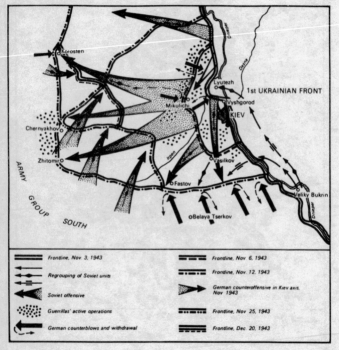

▬▬▬ Frontline, Nov. 3, 1943	▬▬▬ Frontline, Nov. 6, 1943
◀━▬ Regrouping of Soviet units	▬▬▬ Frontline, Nov. 12, 1943
◀━ Soviet offensive	▶━ German counteroffensive in Kiev axis, Nov 1943
∴∴∴ Guerrillas' active operations	▬▬▬ Frontline, Nov. 25, 1943
◀━ German counterblows and withdrawal	▬▬▬ Frontline, Dec. 20, 1943

The Korsun-Shevechenkovsky Pocket   No. 8

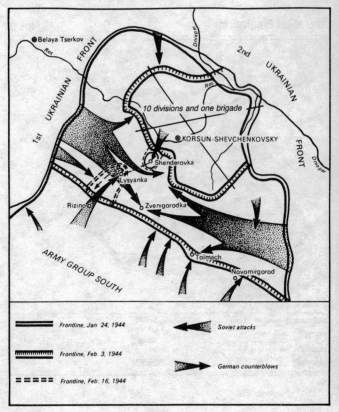

Belaya Tserkov

1st UKRAINIAN FRONT

2nd UKRAINIAN FRONT

Ros

Dnieper

10 divisions and one brigade

KORSUN-SHEVCHENKOVSKY

Shenderovka

Lysyanka

Rizino

Zvenigorodka

ARMY GROUP SOUTH

Tolmach

Novomirgorod

▬▬▬ Frontline, Jan. 24, 1944	◀■ Soviet attacks
▮▮▮▮ Frontline, Feb. 3, 1944	
==== Frontline, Feb. 16, 1944	▶ German counterblows

Operation Bagration

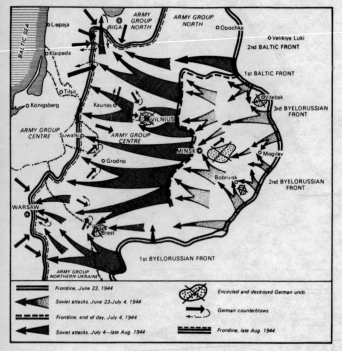

▰▰▰ Frontline, June 23, 1944	Encircled and destroyed German units
◀━ Soviet attacks, June 23-July 4, 1944	German counterblows
▰ ▰ ▰ Frontline, end of day, July 4, 1944	
◀━ Soviet attacks, July 4—late Aug. 1944	▰▰▰ Frontline, late Aug 1944

Liberation of the Crimea No. 10

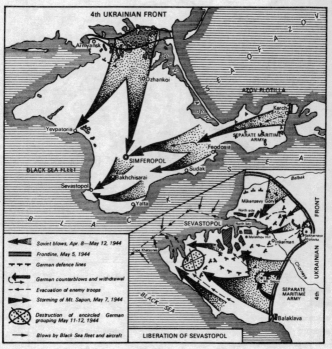

4th UKRAINIAN FRONT

Armyansk
Dzhankoi
SEA OF AZOV
AZOV FLOTILLA
Kerch
Yevpatoria
SEPARATE MARITIME ARMY
Feodosia
BLACK SEA FLEET
SIMFEROPOL
Sudak
Bakhchisarai
Sevastopol
Yalta
BLACK SEA

LIBERATION OF SEVASTOPOL

Belbek
Mikenzevy Gory
North side
North Jetty
SEVASTOPOL
Malakhov Hill
Inkerman
Sakharnaya Golovka
Cape Khersones
Mt. Sapun
SEPARATE MARITIME ARMY
Chorgun
4th UKRAINIAN FRONT
Balaklava

Soviet blows, Apr. 8—May 12, 1944

Frontline, May 5, 1944

German defence lines

German counterblows and withdrawal

Evacuation of enemy troops

Storming of Mt. Sapun, May 7, 1944

Destruction of encircled German grouping May 11-12, 1944

Blows by Black Sea fleet and aircraft

Towards the Balkans

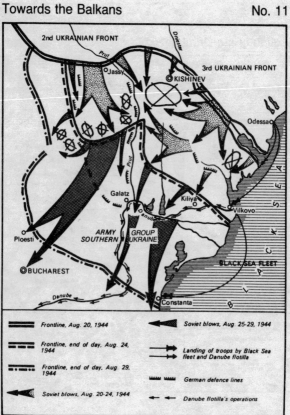

▬▬▬ *Frontline, Aug. 20, 1944*	◀▬▬ *Soviet blows, Aug. 25-29, 1944*
▬ ▬ ▬ *Frontline, end of day, Aug. 24, 1944*	
▬·▬·▬ *Frontline, end of day, Aug. 29, 1944*	▶▶ *Landing of troops by Black Sea fleet and Danube flotilla*
◀▬▬ *Soviet blows, Aug. 20-24, 1944*	┅┅┅ *German defence lines*
	◀‑ ◀‑ *Danube flotilla's operations*

Breakthrough to the Baltic

No. 12

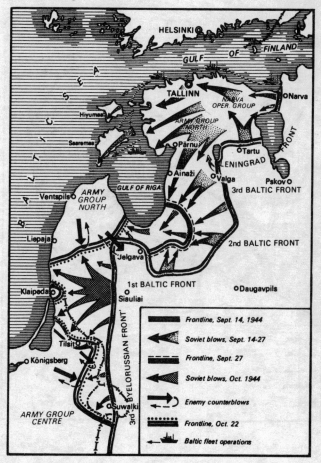

HELSINKI

GULF OF FINLAND

BALTIC SEA

TALLINN

NARVA OPER GROUP

ONarva

Hiyumaa

ARMY GROUP NORTH

Saaremaa

Pärnu

OTartu

LENINGRAD

Valga

FRONT

Ainaži

Pskov O

3rd BALTIC FRONT

GULF OF RIGA

Ventspils

ARMY GROUP NORTH

2nd BALTIC FRONT

Liepaja

Jelgava

1st BALTIC FRONT

O Daugavpils

Klaipeda

Siauliai

BYELORUSSIAN FRONT

Tilsit

Königsberg

ARMY GROUP CENTRE

Suwalki

3rd

▰▰▰	Frontline, Sept. 14, 1944
◀	Soviet blows, Sept. 14-27
▬ ▬ ▬	Frontline, Sept. 27
◀	Soviet blows, Oct. 1944
⇦	Enemy counterblows
••••••	Frontline, Oct. 22
⛴	Baltic fleet operations

The Storming of Königsberg

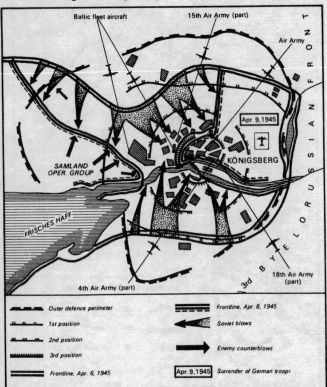

Baltic fleet aircraft

15th Air Army (part)

Air Army

3rd BYELORUSSIAN FRONT

Apr. 9, 1945

KÖNIGSBERG

SAMLAND OPER. GROUP

FRISCHES HAFF

4th Air Army (part)

18th Air Army (part)

Outer defence perimeter	Frontline, Apr. 8, 1945
1st position	Soviet blows
2nd position	
3rd position	Enemy counterblows
Frontline, Apr. 6, 1945	Apr. 9, 1945 Surrender of German troops

The Capture of Budapest   No. 14

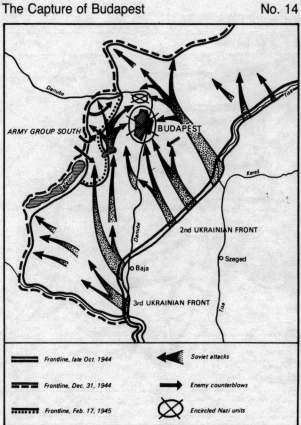

Frontline, late Oct. 1944

Frontline, Dec. 31, 1944

Frontline, Feb. 17, 1945

Soviet attacks

Enemy counterblows

Encircled Nazi units

The Fall of Berlin   No. 15

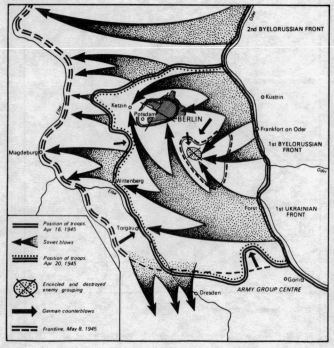

In the Far East   No. 16

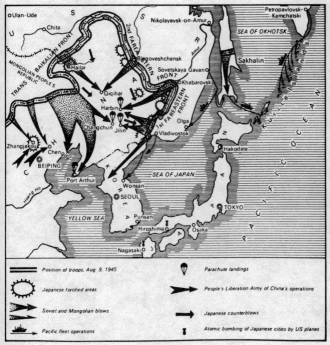

Position of troops, Aug. 9, 1945		Parachute landings
Japanese fortified areas		People's Liberation Army of China's operations
Soviet and Mongolian blows		Japanese counterblows
Pacific fleet operations		Atomic bombing of Japanese cities by US planes

Victory

Byelorussian Front entered Poland and liberated the city of Lublin.

Operation Bagration was one of the biggest in the Second World War. It resulted in the rout of 67 enemy divisions and three brigades. The Nazi Command was forced to shift troops from Western Europe to the east, which facilitated the operations of the Anglo-American Allies on the Second Front in France.

The entire territory of Byelorussia, parts of Lithuania and Latvia, and Polish lands east of the Vistula River were liberated from the Nazis, and the front approached Eastern Prussia.

MAP No. 10

By April 1944 almost the whole of the Ukraine west of the Dnieper had been liberated from the Nazis. But in the rear of the Soviet Army, in the Crimean Peninsula, there still remained a large enemy grouping of 12 divisions and about 30 separate units, a total of 200,000 men, 3,600 guns and mortars, and 215 tanks.

The Soviet Command ordered the forces of the Fourth Ukrainian Front, jointly with the Separate Maritime Army and the Black Sea Fleet, to destroy the enemy by a swift blow and liberated the Crimea.

The Soviet offensive began on April 8. The main blow was being struck from the Sivash Bay. The engineers built two 3-km bridges across the bay in difficult conditions. The heavily fortified enemy positions were broken through, the German soldiers faltered, and soon their retreat became a flight. At the same time Soviet divisions broke into the Crimea from the Perekop Isthmus. Units of the Separate Maritime Army captured Kerch in the east of the peninsula. The enemy began retreating toward Sevastopol along the coast.

In mid-April the Soviet troops reached Sevastopol. The

German troops found themselves in a hopeless situation. But Hitler ordered that the city be held at all costs.

The storming of Sevastopol began on May 5. In two days the forward line of defense was broken through. Street fighting began; it was especially fierce on a high ground named Sapun-Gora. The German soldiers could not withstand the onslaught of Soviet assault groups and surrendered one position after another. On May 9 Sevastopol was completely liberated.

Whereas in 1941–1942 the Wehrmacht needed 250 days to capture the Crimea and Sevastopol, the Soviet Army in 1944 broke through the powerful enemy fortifications in the Crimea in 35 days. To storm and take Sevastopol the Soviet units needed only five days.

The Soviet offensive in the Crimea was completed on May 12. The remains of the enemy grouping were captured. Those who tried to escape by boat were sunk. The Crimean debacle cost Nazi generals 100,000 officers and men and the entire materiel of the 17th Army. Soviet troops came close to the Balkans and the Carpathians. The Black Sea Fleet now threatened Romania, one of Germany's satellites, and controlled Bosporus and Dardanelles.

Eight months later a historic conference of the leaders of three great powers—Stalin, Roosevelt, and Churchill—was held in Yalta, in the Crimea. The conference adopted important decisions on postwar arrangements. They were to guarantee universal peace and international security.

MAP No. 11

In the summer of 1944 the Soviet Army reached the Romanian borders. The Soviet Command planned a Jassy-Kishinev operation, whose purpose was to encircle and destroy Army Group South Ukraine, and to force Romania to withdraw from the war. The operation was to be carried out by the Second and Third Ukrainian fronts. They were to be supported by the Black Sea Fleet and the Danube River Flotilla.

The offensive began at dawn on August 20. For one and a half hours the ground was shaking from the explosions of artillery and mortar shells. Thick smoke rose above the enemy defenses. The artillery was still firing when two air armies started bombing the Germans. The Nazi generals lost control of the troops. Although the enemy defenses were largely destroyed, separate units rendered stubborn resistance. A Soviet tank army was sent into the gap. The Nazi Command was trying to contain the attack by bringing in reserves. But they were destroyed by powerful blows delivered by aircraft and tanks when the reserves were still on march. Soviet divisions achieved freedom of operational maneuver.

The offensive of the Third Ukrainian Front from a springboard south of Kishinev was developing successfully as well. On the very first day of the offensive the enemy defenses were broken through. Two tank corps were brought into the gap.

The troops of the two fronts were converging at a rapid pace. On August 24 they closed the ring of encirclement, and 18 enemy divisions were caught in a trap. The encircled Nazis rendered stiff resistance. They made repeated attempts to break out to the west, but all their attempts failed. On August 27 the Nazi main forces on the left bank of the Prut River stopped their resistance. Only a small grouping on the right bank of the river managed to break out of the trap. It tried to force its way to the Carpathians, but was again encircled and destroyed.

The Soviet troops in Romania advanced to the west and south. Pressed against the Black Sea, the main forces of the Romanian Royal Army laid down their arms. The Soviet Army's victory at Jassy and Kishinev triggered off a people's revolution in Romania. On August 23 an uprising broke out in Bucharest. The fascist dictatorship was overthrown. The new government not only canceled Romania's alliance with Germany but declared war on it. About half a million Romanian troops joined the forces of the Third Ukrainian Front.

For the successful Jassy-Kishinev operation the commanders of the two fronts, Malinovsky and Tolbukhin, were promoted to the rank of marshal.

MAP No. 12

The liberation of the Baltic republics—Estonia, Lithuania, and Latvia—started in the autumn of 1944. A quarter of all the Wehrmacht forces in the east was concentrated there—59 divisions. They found themselves cut off from the main German forces.

The First Baltic Front commanded by General Bagramyan gained the greatest initial success. Its divisions broke through the powerful enemy defenses and reached the West Dvina River south of Riga. Nazi units struck two powerful counterblows, but the Soviet forces parried them. From the east the Germans were being pressed by divisions of other Soviet fronts. After regrouping the armies of the Leningrad front struck a powerful blow against the enemy at Tartu. On September 22 they liberated Tallinn, the capital of the Estonian Republic.

At the same time General Bagramyan regrouped the forces of his front and shifted the main blow from the Riga sector to Klaipeda (Memel). His front began the offensive on October 5. Five days later Soviet tank brigades reached the Baltic coast south of Klaipeda. The main forces of German Army Group North were cut off from Eastern Prussia.

Divisions of the Second and Third Baltic fronts were advancing on Riga. They struck blows from three directions on October 13 and beat the enemy off from the right-bank part of the city, and two days later captured all of Riga. In the southern part of the Baltic area the troops of the First Baltic Front, together with the forces of the Third Byelorussian Front, assault-crossed the Nieman and penetrated deep into Eastern Prussia.

After these battles Estonia, Lithuania, and most of Latvia were liberated. The war was now fought on the territory of Nazi Germany. Army Group North suffered a debacle, as a result of which 29 German divisions were routed. West of Riga, in Kurland, 41 German divisions found themselves in a trap. The fighting there continued till the end of the war. After Nazi Germany's capitulation 190,000 German officers and men, including 42 generals, surrendered to the Soviet troops in that area.

MAP No. 13

In early 1945 the Soviet Command carried out a major operation in Eastern Prussia. Its purpose was to cut off the German troops from the main forces in Germany and destroy them.

A dense fog hung over the battlefield on the day of the offensive, January 13, so that the aircraft could not take off. After a two-hour artillery preparation the infantry, supported by tanks, went into the attack. The enemy was resisting fiercely. In many years the Germans had built there a great number of reinforced concrete weapon emplacements and dug many kilometers of trenches. The thick-walled stone buildings had been turned into fortresses.

Breaking down enemy defenses, the Soviet troops were slowly but persistently advancing. On January 19 they captured Tilsit, and two days later Gumbinnen. Fearing an encirclement, the Nazi generals began withdrawing their troops. Three Soviet armies and tank units pursued them. A large Wehrmacht grouping became isolated. After a brief tactical respite the Soviet troops proceeded to destroy them. In early April the whole grouping was routed; almost 100,000 German soldiers were killed and 50,000 taken prisoner.

In one of the pitched battles front commander General Chernyakhovsky was mortally wounded. Marshal Vasilevsky replaced him.

The Soviet troops were now poised for attack on Königsberg. The city was heavily fortified. Two rings of strongpoints had been built around it. The garrison comprised 130,000 men, about 4,000 artillery pieces, and 100 tanks. Nazi generals forced even civilians to carry arms and defend the city.

The storming of Königsberg began in the morning on April 6. Thousands of artillery and mortar shells were poured on the fortifications. Also, three air armies and long-range aircraft units were continuously bombing them. The city's defensive system had been broken up by evening. The garrison of each fort now fought at its own initiative. Soviet soldiers pressed forward through the fire, smoke, and dust. Reinforced concrete fortifications came down with a crash and fires broke out at many points. The artillery stopped firing because the troops were now in too close a contact. Hand-to-hand fighting broke out everywhere. By the end of the fourth day of continuous fighting Königsberg fell.

After the war Königsberg and the area around it were ceded to the Soviet Union by decision of the Potsdam Conference of the leaders of three great powers. The city was renamed Kaliningrad in honor of Mikhail Kalinin, who was the Soviet President from 1919 to 1946.

MAP No. 14

In the autumn of 1944 Hungary remained the only ally of Nazi Germany. The leaders of the Third Reich made every effort to keep it under their thumb, to use the country's resources for war production and its manpower for fighting on the war fronts. But Soviet troops were advancing on all sides and further resistance involved unnecessary casualties. Realizing this, the Hungarian Command sent a delegation to Moscow to negotiate a truce. Hitler, however, deposed the Hungarian government and brought to power one of his henchmen, Szalasy, a fascist, who ordered the troops to continue fighting.

In late October the Soviet Army began its Budapest operation. After two months of fierce fighting the Soviet forces closed the ring of encirclement 80 km north of Budapest. About 200,000 enemy soldiers were trapped in it.

The encircled troops were presented with an ultimatum, offering humane terms for their surrender. The Nazis killed the Soviet truce emissaries. This treacherous murder evoked anger and indignation among many peoples of the world.

In early January 1945 Soviet divisions began eliminating the encircled enemy grouping. The fighting became protracted. The Nazi Command made three attempts to rescue its troops and restore the defenses on the Danube. Fierce fighting was raging in the city. Almost every house had to be taken by storm. The Soviet Command did not use heavy artillery and aircraft in order to avoid the destruction of historical documents and cultural values. The Nazis and Szalasy's men established a reign of terror in the city— they shot civilians on the slightest suspicion.

Despite the enemy's stubborn resistance the ring of encirclement was tightening every day. Romanian soldiers, Hungarian guerrillas, and about 2,500 Hungarian servicemen who had come over to the side of the Soviet Army were fighting side by side with Soviet soldiers.

On the morning of February 13 the last pockets of enemy resistance were crushed. The remnants of the encircled units and the commander of the grouping surrendered. The fascist regime that had ruled Hungary for many years had collapsed. Nazi Germany had lost its last ally and now was completely isolated.

MAP No. 15

The war was coming to an end. The Nazi Command stopped the resistance on the western front almost completely. It threw all its forces to the eastern front. Berlin was being defended by about a million officers and men who had 10,400 guns and mortars, 1,500 tanks, and 3,300 planes.

The Soviet Command assigned the forces of three fronts to capture the capital of the Third Reich. They comprised 2.5 million men, about 42,000 guns and mortars, over 6,200 tanks and self-propelled guns, and 7,500 aircraft. The Soviet superiority in manpower and arms was considerable, but in the directions of the main blows the Soviet Command achieved a superiority that was much greater.

The Soviet offensive began before dawn on April 16. Powerful searchlights were switched on and thousands of guns and mortars began firing. In the glare of searchlights, which blinded the German troops, the Soviet infantry and tanks went into the attack. After five days of heavy fighting, Soviet regiments reached the outskirts of Berlin. At the same time other Soviet units were closing the ring of encirclement around the city. On April 25 units of the First Ukrainian Front linked up with American troops near Torgau on the bank of the Elbe River. Soviet troops met up with Anglo-American units in other areas as well.

The last storming of the central districts of Germany's capital began on April 26. The blows were being struck from different directions, converging on the center of the city. The enemy was offering fierce resistance. Each street and each house had to be taken by storm. Late on April 30, the Reichstag was captured. Hitler and Goebbels committed suicide. On May 2 the Berlin garrison surrendered. The capital of Nazi Germany fell.

Three days later the citizens of Prague staged an uprising. With their active assistance Soviet troops liberated the

city from Nazi occupation. On May 8 an act of the unconditional surrender of Nazi Germany was signed in Berlin.
The guns became silent in Europe.

The victory of the Soviet people over Nazism, a victory
to which no small contribution was made by the other
peoples of the countries of the anti-Hitler coalition, saved
the world from the brown plague. It signified the victory
of freedom-loving democratic forces, and had a strong
impact on the further progressive development of mankind.

MAP No. 16

The victory over Nazi Germany did not yet extinguish
the flames of the Second World War. Militarist Japan still
waged hostilities in the Far East and in the Pacific.

Loyal to its Allies, the Soviet Union began military
operations against Japan in order to bring an end to the war
closer and save hundreds of thousands of human lives. The
Mongolian People's Republic declared war on Japan at the
same time.

The strongest grouping of Japanese land forces was
concentrated in Manchuria on the border with the USSR. It
comprised 1.2 million officers and men, about 5,400 artillery pieces, 1,200 tanks, and 1,800 planes. Two other
armies were positioned near Peking.

The Soviet Command formed three fronts in the Far
East: the Transbaikal, First Far Eastern, and Second Far
Eastern Fronts. Marshal Vasilevsky was appointed Commander of all the armed forces in the region. The three
fronts had 1.5 million officers and men, over 26,000 guns
and mortars, about 5,300 tanks and self-propelled guns,
and more than 5,000 aircraft. They were supported by the
ships of the Pacific Fleet and the Amur River Flotilla.

At dawn on August 9 the forces of the Transbaikal Front
stormed the Great Khingan. Bypassing fortified areas and
leaving behind the enemy's centers of resistance, they

were swiftly moving forward. Three days later Soviet divisions reached the Manchurian Plain in the rear of the main forces of the Japanese Army.

At the same time the forces of the First Far Eastern Front were quickly advancing from the east and the forces of the Second Far Eastern Front from the north. Seaborne and airborne troops were landed in strategically important towns and populated localities. The main forces of the Japanese Kwantung Army became cut off. Their headquarters had lost control and communication with the retreating units. Realizing the futility of resistance, the Japanese Command declared its surrender on August 19. The troops were laying down arms and surrendered en masse. Over 500,000 men were taken prisoner.

After the capitulation of the Kwantung Army, Japan could not continue the war any longer. On September 2, its representatives signed an act of unconditional capitulation on board the USS *Missouri* in the Tokyo Bay.

The Second World War ended in the complete rout of fascism and militarism. During that war mankind suffered tremendous losses: 55 million killed and 90 million wounded; tens of thousands of towns and cities and hundreds of thousands of villages were destroyed. The grim results of the Second World War must not be forgotten by the present generation or the generations to come.

MAP No. 17

After its debacle at Kursk in the summer of 1943 the German Army could not regain its strength. A sweeping offensive of Soviet troops began. The liberation of the Northern Caucasus and the Donbas in the Ukraine, the assault-crossing of the Dnieper, and the establishment of bridgeheads on its right bank were the main battles in late 1943.

The year 1944 began with a major Soviet offensive at

Leningrad. The blockade of the city was completely lifted and a sizable part of Estonia was liberated. Then came the blows in southern Ukraine. In May the Crimea and Odessa were liberated and in June, Karelia. The Soviet offensive was being conducted throughout the entire front, from the Barents in the north to the Black Sea in the south. Within a single operation the depth of penetration by Soviet divisions had reached from 150 to 500 km.

In June 1944 the Anglo-American forces opened a second front by landing in France. However, even after that the main events took place in the east. The Wehrmacht was keeping up to 60 divisions in Western Europe and over 200 divisions in the east. In those days Stalin wrote to Roosevelt and Churchill: "The general offensive will develop by stages, through consecutive engagement of the armies in offensive operations."

Two weeks after the Allied landing in Normandy the Soviet troops began carrying out the biggest operation of the Second World War, Operation Bagration in Byelorussia. They broke through to the Vistula in Poland and crossed the river. By the autumn the Ukraine, Byelorussia, Moldavia, and a large part of the Baltic republics had been liberated.

Retreating, the Nazis destroyed industrial enterprises, houses, bridges, and railways. Tremendous damage was done to agriculture. But hardly had the guns stopped firing and smoke dispersed over the ruins, when the Soviet people got down to restoring what had been damaged.

After a series of blows by the Soviet Army the Wehrmacht troops were thrown far back westward. Taking up advantageous positions, the Soviet regiments were ready for a new offensive. The liberations of the European nations from the Nazi invaders began. They were thrown out of Romania, Bulgaria, and Yugoslavia. Great territories in Poland, Czechoslovakia, and Hungary were liberated.

The year 1945 saw the final victories of the Soviet armed forces. In January they launched a new large-scale offensive on a front from the Baltic to the Carpathians.

The enemy was thrown back from the Vistula to the Oder. This offensive helped the Anglo-American troops to avoid a debacle in the Ardennes at the hands of the German forces.

Finally in April the war reached the very walls of Berlin. After a short but fierce storming of the capital of the Third Reich, Berlin fell. Nazi Germany surrendered.

1. The War Begins:

June 22, 1941

Marshal of the Soviet Union Georgi Zhukov (1896–1974) had served in the army since 1915. During the Second World War, he was the Chief of the General Staff of the Soviet Army, the commander of a number of fronts, and a Deputy Supreme Commander.

After the war, he was the commander of the troops of military districts, a Deputy Minister and the Minister of Defense of the Soviet Union.

When war broke out in 1941, he was the Chief of the General Staff of the Soviet Army.

On June 21, 1941, all the personnel of the general staff and the Defense Ministry were ordered to stay on the job overnight. It was necessary to ensure prompt transmission to the districts of the Defense Commissar's directive ordering maximum combat preparedness of border troops. Meanwhile, the Minister of Defense and I were conducting incessant telephone conversations with the district commanders and their chiefs of staff, who reported increasing noise on the other side of the border from the border guards and forward covering units.

At about midnight, Commander of the Kiev District Kirponos reported over the telephone from his command post at Ternopol that a German soldier had appeared in our lines, that he swam across the river, presented himself to our border guards, and told them that the German forces were going to mount an offensive at 4:00 A.M. Kirponos was ordered to speed up transmission to all units of the directive calling for alert status.

Everything now indicated that the German forces were moving up to the frontier. At half-past midnight, we notified Stalin, who asked whether the directive had been sent to all districts. I replied that it had.

Near dawn on June 22, General Vatutin and I were in the office of the Minister of Defense Marshal Timoshenko.

At 3:30 A.M. the Chief of Staff of the Western District General Klimovskikh reported about a German air raid on towns in Byelorussia. About three minutes later, General Purkayev, the chief of staff of the Kiev District, reported about an air strike on Ukrainian towns. At 3:40 A.M., General Kuznetsov, the Commander of the Baltic District, called to report about enemy air raids on Kaunas and other towns.

The Minister of Defense ordered me to phone Stalin. I started calling. No one answered. I kept calling. Finally I heard the sleep-dulled voice of the general on duty of the security section. I asked him to call Stalin to the phone.

About three minutes later, Stalin picked up the receiver.

I reported the situation and requested permission to start retaliation. Stalin was silent. The only thing I could hear was the sound of his breathing.

"Do you understand me?"

Silence again.

At last Stalin asked, "Where is the minister?"

"Talking with the Kiev District on the telephone."

"Come to the Kremlin with Timoshenko. Tell my secretary to summon all Politburo members."

Marshal Timoshenko and I came to the Kremlin. All the

Politburo members were assembled. Stalin, his face white, was sitting at the table cradling a tobacco-filled pipe in his hand.

After some time, he said, "We must phone the German embassy immediately."

The embassy replied that Ambassador Count von der Schulenburg was anxious to deliver an urgent message.

Minister of Foreign Affairs Molotov was authorized to receive the ambassador.

Meanwhile, First Deputy Chief of Staff General Vatutin had passed word that, following a strong artillery barrage on several sectors in the northwest and west, German land forces had mounted an assault.

A while later, Molotov hastened into the office and said, "The German government has declared war on us."

Stalin sank down into his chair and lost himself in thought.

There was a long and pregnant pause.

I decided to risk breaking the seemingly everlasting silence and suggested crashing down upon the attackers immediately with the full strength of our border districts to hold up any further advance by the enemy.

"Issue a directive," Stalin said.

By 8:00 A.M. on June 22 the general staff established that:

- there had been a powerful enemy bomb strike at many airfields in the Western, Kiev, and Baltic Special Military Districts, where serious damage had been inflicted on our aircraft, which had no time to take off and disperse to field airstrips;

- many towns and railway junctions in the Baltic area, Byelorussia, and the Ukraine, together with naval bases at Sevastopol and on the Baltic coast, had also been bombed;

- bitter fighting was going on against German land forces along our entire Western frontier. In many sectors, the Germans had engaged forward units of the Red Army.

On June 22 the Baltic, Western, and Kiev Special Military Districts were transformed into the Northwestern, Western, and Southwestern fronts.

At about 1:00 P.M. on June 22 Stalin telephoned me to say, "Our front commanders lack combat experience and evidently they have become somewhat confused. The Politburo has decided to send you to the Southwestern Front as a representative of the General Headquarters of the Supreme Command. We are also sending Shaposhnikov and Kulik to the Western Front. I have seen them and given them instructions. You must fly to Kiev at once and then proceed to the front headquarters at Ternopol."

By the end of the day I was in Kiev. It was dangerous to go any farther by air. German airmen were chasing our transport planes. We would have to go by car. Having received the latest news on the situation from Vatutin, I left for Ternopol where Colonel-General Kirponos, now commander of the Southwestern Front, had his command post.

We arrived at the command post late at night, and I immediately got in touch with Vatutin on the telephone.

Here is what he told me:

"By the end of June 22, despite vigorous measures, the general staff had failed to receive accurate information about our forces or the enemy from front, army, and air-force headquarters. Information on the depth of the enemy penetration into our territory is quite contradictory. There are no precise data on losses in aviation and land forces. It is known only that the aviation of the Byelorussian District had sustained very great losses. The general staff cannot get in touch with front commanders Kuznetsov and Pavlov, who had gone out to their troops. The headquarters of these fronts did not know where their commanders were at that moment."

According to air-reconnaissance data, battles were being fought in the areas of our fortified zones and nearly 10 to 12 miles inside our territory. Attempts by front headquarters to contact the troops had no success, as there was neither cable nor radio communication with most of the armies and some of the corps.

By 9:00 A.M. on the following day we arrived at the command post of the commander of the 8th Mechanized Corps, General Ryabyshev. I knew him well from our service in the Kiev Special Military District. It was easy to guess by the look of the corps commander and his staff officers that they had come a long, hard way. They had, in fact, moved very swiftly from the Drogobych area to the area of Brody, and were in high spirits.

Ryabyshev showed me on the map where and how the corps was being deployed. He reported briefly on the condition of the units.

"The corps requires one day for complete concentration, checking of materiel and replenishment of stocks," he said. "Within that time there will be a reconnaissance in force and a control system will be organized. Therefore, the corps will be capable of going into action in full strength by the morning of June 24."

"Good," I said. "It would, of course, be better to deliver a counterblow together with the 9th, 19th, and 22nd Mechanized Corps, but unfortunately they are late in arriving at their areas of departure. The situation will not allow us to wait for the complete deployment of the corps. In executing its counterblow, the 8th Mechanized Corps may be expected to come up against a powerful enemy tank and anti-tank artillery screen. Considering this, there must be a thorough reconnaissance of the terrain and of the enemy forces."

Having settled all cardinal issues with the corps commander, by nightfall we were back in Ternopol at the front command post.

Lieutenant-General Purkayev, Front Chief of Staff, and Colonel-General Kirponos, the front commander, reported:

"There is fighting in all sectors of the front. The major—and exceedingly bitter—battle is being fought in the area of Brody-Dubno-Vladimir-Volynsky. The 9th and 19th Mechanized Corps will be assembling in the forests in the area of Rovno on June 25."

"We have decided," the front commander continued, "not to await the complete concentration of the corps, but to mount a counterattack at Klevan and Dubno on June 24. Besides the 22nd Mechanized Corps, the commander of the 5th Army must pool the actions of the 9th and 19th Mechanized Corps and provide them with the necessary assistance."

It was a reasonable decision, and I agreed with the front command, suggesting, however, that they verify liaison between the corps and the front aviation.

On June 24 Ryabyshev's 8th Mechanized Corps mounted an offensive toward Berestechko. We pinned great hopes on this corps. It had been better equipped with the latest tanks than the others and was fairly well trained. The 15th Mechanized Corps under General Karpezo was advancing east of Radekhov. The attack by these corps and, in particular, the successful action of the 8th Mechanized Corps soon had a telling effect on the German forces. This was especially true after the rout of the 57th Infantry Division, which had been covering the right flank of the 48th Motorized Corps of von Kleist's group.

A rather grave situation developed that day for the German 48th Motorized Corps. The Nazis were compelled to throw in all their aviation against our counterblow, and this alone saved their units from utter defeat. They were forced to bring up the 44th Army Corps and other units.

While at the command post of the Southwestern Front, we naturally devoted our prime attention to the Dubno sector, the center of major fighting in the Ukraine.

From telephone conversations with the 6th Army Commander, General Muzychenko, and the 26th Army Commander, General Kostenko, I learned that the advancing German 17th Army had leveled its major blow in the direction of Lvov.

The Command of the 17th German Army had deployed five infantry divisions in this sector. Despite heavy artillery fire, air strikes, and sustained attacks, enemy forces had been unsuccessful in their efforts to capture the Rava-Russkaya fortified zone and break the resistance of the 41st Infantry Division. In the afternoon and evening of June 22 the 41st Division, which had two artillery regiments, was reinforced additionally with the 209th Corps Artillery Regiment armed with 152-mm guns. On that day enemy forces sustained great losses without achieving any success.

The Peremyshl fortified area was held by the 52nd and the 150th independent machine-gun battalions and the 92nd Border Guard Detachment. They had occupied their emplacements by 6:00 in the morning of June 22. Together with the border-guard troops and armed volunteer detachments, they were the first to stand up to the enemy fire and attacks.

For several hours the brave defenders of the city repelled the onslaught of a superior enemy force. Then the commander of the border-guard detachment ordered them to withdraw beyond the city limits, where they once again stopped the enemy. In the meantime, the 99th Infantry Division under Colonel Dementiev approached Peremyshl. On June 23, jointly with a composite border-guard battalion, it delivered a counterblow and threw the enemy out of the city.

On June 23 the Germans renewed their attacks, which were particularly severe in the Rava-Russkaya sector. In some places enemy units succeeded in penetrating the 41st Division's defenses, but thanks to firm control by General Mikushev, the enemy was thrown back to his starting point by a successful counterattack.

However, by the close of June 23, the enemy dealt a powerful blow at the junction between the Rava-Russkaya and Peremyshl areas, defended by the 97th and 159th infantry divisions. The latter, which was then being deployed, had considerable numbers of untrained reservists in its ranks and, unable to withstand enemy attacks, began a withdrawal, thus gravely endangering adjacent units. The countermeasures undertaken by the 6th Army commander General Muzychenko failed to remedy the situation and by the close of June 24 the gap in the defenses reached 25 miles.

On June 25–26, the fighting continued with mounting intensity. The enemy threw in a powerful air force. Fierce battles were fought in the air and on the ground. Both sides were suffering heavy losses. Frequently the German airmen would simply break down in the face of bold blows by our pilots and withdraw to their airfields.

Following the appearance of forward enemy units in the Dubno area, General Ryabyshev was ordered to turn his 8th Corps to confront them. The 15th Mechanized Corps was spearheading its main forces in the general direction of Berestechko and then on toward Dubno. The approaching 36th Infantry and 19th Mechanized Corps were also proceeding to the Dubno area. Fierce fighting in the Dubno area began on June 27.

The Germans reinforced their troops with the 55th Army Corps, and this alone saved the Dubno group of enemy forces from a complete rout. Sustaining heavy losses, the enemy was compelled to withdraw his forces from other sectors and move them toward Dubno.

Our troops were unable to smash the enemy and stop his advance altogether, but the main job had been done: the enemy strike force which had been thrusting toward Kiev was held up in the Brody-Dubno area and weakened seriously.

From my phone talks with General Vatutin during those days, I was aware that on the Western and Northwestern fronts the commanding generals and their staffs still had no reliable communications with the army commanders. Our divisions and corps had to fight in isolation, without cooperation with the neighboring troops and aviation, and without proper direction from above. From Vatutin's reports, it became clear to me that an exceptionally difficult situation had developed at the Western and Northwestern fronts.

Vatutin told me that Stalin was nervous and tending to blame it all on the command of the Western Front and its staff, and that he was castigating Marshal Kulik for inactivity. It became known from dispatches sent in by Marshal Shaposhnikov, who was at the headquarters of the Western front, that Kulik had been at the headquarters of the 3rd Army on the morning of June 23 but communications with it had been cut off.

Sometime later, however, the general staff managed to establish from various sources that large-scale groups of Panzer and mechanized forces had broken through in several sectors of those fronts and were moving swiftly into Byelorussia and the Baltic area.

In those days, neither the front commands, nor the General Headquarters of the Supreme Command, nor the general staff had any complete information about the enemy forces deployed against our fronts. The general staff was receiving plainly exaggerated intelligence from the fronts about the enemy's tank, air, and motorized units. Today, when we possess almost exhaustive information on the forces of both sides, we can take stock of the grouping of Soviet forces in the border military districts and then of the deployment of the German forces which invaded our country, to gain a complete picture of the situation in the first days of the war.

Stationed over a vast territory were 170 Soviet divisions with a frontage of over 2,100 miles. Along the land border, the Soviet troops were in different groupings of unequal strength, depending on the local conditions and the tactical and operational importance of a given sector. On the eve of the war, these forces were stationed as follows:

The Baltic Special Military District (Commander: Colonel-General Kuznetsov) had 25 divisions and one infantry brigade, including 4 tank and 2 motorized divisions.

The Western Special Military District (Commander: General of the Army Pavlov) had 24 infantry divisions, 12 tank, 6 motorized, and 2 cavalry divisions.

The Kiev Special Military District (Commander: Colonel-General Kirponos) had 32 infantry, 16 tank, 8 motorized, and 2 cavalry divisions.

The Odessa Military District (Commander: Lieutenant-General Cherevichenko) had 13 infantry, 4 tank, 2 motorized, and 3 cavalry divisions.

The High Command of the German troops sent 153 divisions into action, including 29 against the Baltic, 50 (including 15 Panzer divisions) against the Western Special, 33 (including 9 Panzer and motorized divisions) against the Kiev Special District, 12 against the Odessa District, and 5 divisions were placed in Finland. Twenty-four divisions were in reserve and advanced along the major strategic directions.

In its Army Groups North, Center, and South, the enemy sent about 4,300 tanks and assault guns into action. The land forces were supported by 4,980 combat aircraft. The assault force had an almost twofold superiority over our artillery. The enemy's artillery was mostly motorized.

On June 26 Stalin phoned me at the command post of the Southwestern Front in Ternopol: "A bad situation has developed on the Western Front. The enemy has approached Minsk. I don't understand what's happening to Pavlov. Nobody knows where Marshal Kulik is. Marshal Shaposhnikov is ill. Can you fly to Moscow at once?"

"I'll discuss further action with generals Kirponos and Purkayev right away, and then go to the airfield."

Late in the evening of June 26, I landed in Moscow and was taken to Stalin straight from the airport. In Stalin's office I saw Marshal Timoshenko and Lieutenant-General Vatutin, my First Deputy, standing stiffly at attention. Both of them were pale and drawn, their eyes red from lack of sleep. Stalin was not in his best mood.

With a brief nod, he said, "Put your heads together and

tell me what can be done in this situation." And he flung on the table a map showing the situation on the Western Front.

I told him we would need about forty minutes to analyze the situation.

"Very well. Report to me in forty minutes."

We went out into an adjoining room and began discussing the situation and our capabilities on the Western Front.

The situation there was indeed highly critical. The remnants of the 3rd and 10th armies were surrounded and fighting an unequal battle, tying down sizable enemy forces west of Minsk. Some units of the 4th Army had withdrawn partially to the Pripyat forests. Scattered formations, which had sustained serious losses in previous battles, were pulling back to the River Berezina from the Dokshitsy-Smolevichi-Slutsk-Pinsk line. These weakened troops of the front were being pursued by powerful enemy concentrations.

Having discussed the situation, we could think of nothing better to suggest than an immediate defensive action on the West Dvina-Polotsk-Vitebsk-Orsha-Mogilev-Mozyr line by the 13th, 19th, 20th, 21st, and 22nd armies. Furthermore, a defense was to be organized immediately on rearward lines running through Selizharovo-Smolensk-Roslavl-Gomel by the 24th and 28th armies of the GHQ reserve. In addition, we proposed the urgent forming of two or three more armies out of divisions of the Moscow Home Guard.

All these proposals were approved by Stalin and went into effect immediately.

In our proposals, we were proceeding from the primary task of building up a defense in depth on the approaches to Moscow, harrying the enemy continuously and checking his advance on one of the lines of defense, then organizing a counteroffensive with troops brought from the Far East and new formations.

In spite of the mass heroism of the officers and men, in spite of the gallant staying power of the commanding officers, the situation in all sectors of the Western Front continued to deteriorate. On the night of June 28 our troops retreated from Minsk.

On June 30 Stalin called me at the general staff headquarters and ordered me to summon General of the Army Pavlov, Commander of the Western Front, to Moscow.

The next day, General Pavlov arrived. I hardly recognized him; he had changed so much in the eight days of the war. That same day he was removed from his command and soon after put on trial. Timoshenko was appointed the Commander of the Western Front and Lieutenant-General Yeremenko his deputy. The armies of the Reserve Front were sent to the front to reinforce it.

On the Northwestern Front, the situation continued to deteriorate drastically.

The 8th and 11th armies, which had escaped encirclement, were now retreating in diverging directions and suffering great losses due to poor organization by the command of the front.

To cover the Pskov–Leningrad direction, the General Headquarters ordered General Lelyushenko, the Commander of the 21st Mechanized Corps, to move out from the Opochka-Idritsa area to the area of Daugavpils and prevent the enemy from forcing the West Dvina River.

This task, however, was clearly impossible to achieve. Already, by June 26, the enemy had forced the West Dvina and captured Daugavpils. Nonetheless, the 21st Mechanized Corps understood a bold counteroffensive, delivering a blow at the 56th German Motorized Corps and checking its advance.

Owing to the belated approach of our reserves to the River Velikaya, the enemy captured the town of Pskov by storm. The 8th Army of the Northwestern Front lost contact with other units and was withdrawing northward.

Thus, in the first eighteen days of the war, the Northwestern Front had lost Lithuania, Latvia, and a portion of the Russian Federation, all of which created the possibility that the enemy would take Luga and draw close to Leningrad, whose approaches were still inadequately fortified and poorly protected.

The battles being fought in early July on the Western Front, in the Vitebsk, Orsha, Mogilev, and Bobruisk sectors were marked by an overwhelming superiority of the enemy's motorized, tank, and air forces. Exhausted by continuous engagements, our troops were pulling back eastward, but even in these circumstances they did their best to inflict maximum casualties on the enemy and hold up his progress as long as possible on the lines of defense.

From Romanian territory, German and Romanian troops went into action against the Southern Front, spearheading their main blow in the direction of Mogilev-Podolsky-Zhmerinka, and creating a threat of an outflanking maneuver against the 12th, 26th, and 6th armies of the Southwestern Front.

In the first six days of intense fighting, the enemy succeeded in breaking through the defenses of the Southern Front and advancing up to 40 miles. The position of the Southwestern Front deteriorated considerably, since at this time, after several attempts, German forces had finally cut through the defenses in the area of Rovno-Dubno-Kremenets and swept into the gap.

On July 4, the German troops approached the Novograd-Volynsky fortified area, where their attacks were beaten off with heavy losses. The enemy motorized and tank units were held up for almost three days. Failing to achieve success, the enemy regrouped his forces south of Novograd-Volynsky. On July 7 the Germans captured Berdichev, and on July 9, Zhitomir.

On the Northern Front, where offensive action had started on June 29, the fighting was local and had no particular influence on the overall strategic situation.

In the early stage of the war, our naval forces had no major engagements with the German navy and were mainly

busy beating off air attacks. However, the Baltic Fleet was
hard put.

The Tallinn base, like the city of Tallinn, was poorly
protected on land due to the unsuccessful action of the 8th
Army of the Northwestern Front. All units of the Baltic
Fleet, together with armed detachments of the city's working people, were thrown into action to defend the capital
of Estonia. Lines of defense and fortifications were built
hastily on the approaches to Tallinn. Key objectives inside
the city were prepared for defense.

In this period, the Northern Fleet acted in cooperation
with the troops of the Northern Front and initiated subma-
rine operations against German shipping's taking nickel
ore out of Petsamo. The Black Sea Fleet primarily ensured
the transportation of manpower and munitions to the maritime armies and struck at enemy lines of communication
by obstructing shipments to Romanian and Bulgarian ports.

Almost three weeks had passed since fascist Germany,
trampling upon the nonaggression pact, invaded our country. During this brief period, the German troops lost about
100,000 men, over 1,000 aircraft, and about half of the
tanks taking part in the offensive.

The Soviet armed forces—especially units of the Western Front—had suffered heavy losses which affected the
subsequent course of events seriously. The balance of
forces in the Soviet-German theater had changed in favor
of the enemy. The enemy had achieved substantial successes, moving up to 300–400 miles inland and capturing
important economic regions and strategic objectives.

Stubborn fighting against the main enemy grouping,
thrusting toward Smolensk, continued in the center of the
front. The units of the 20th Army attacked the enemy
continuously and held the defenses along a wide frontage.
Still, they were unable to contain the 9th German Army,
which bypassed our army and entered the southern part of
the city.

On July 16, 1941, Smolensk was almost wholly occupied by the enemy. The 16th and the 20th armies were encircled in the northern part of the city, but they did not lay down their arms and resisted for nearly ten days. Their action delayed the Germans' advance toward Moscow.

The Battle of Smolensk played an important role in the summer operations of 1941. Although it had been impossible to defeat the enemy, as our General Headquarters had planned, the enemy striking forces had been exhausted. According to German generals, they lost 250,000 officers and men.

After the heavy battles at Smolensk, the fighting abated for a while. Both sides were putting their troops in order and preparing for new battles. However, the fighting in the area of Yelnya did not stop. The Yelnya salient of the front which had been captured by the Germans was a very advantageous bridgehead for striking a blow at Moscow, and the Germans tried to hold it whatever the cost.

The Germans continued to advance toward Leningrad, but in spite of their successes, they could not break through the Soviet defenses and reach the outskirts of Leningrad.

But what was going on at the time in the Ukraine, where the troops of the Southwestern Front were waging a bitter defensive battle?

Capture of the Ukraine was of particular economic importance to the Germans. They wanted to overrun the Ukraine as quickly as possible in order to deprive the Soviet Union of its foremost industrial and agricultural base and simultaneously to boost their own economic potential with Krivoi Rog iron ore, Donets coal, Nikopol manganese, and Ukrainian grain.

Meeting stiff resistance at the Kiev fortified area, the German troops executed a sharp southward maneuver, enveloping our 6th and 12th armies which were withdrawing from the Berdichev-Starokonstantinov-Proskurov line. Part of the enemy forces reached the sector of the 26th Army south of Kiev, but this had no substantial impact because the main enemy force—Army Group South—was moving south at the time. Our 6th and 12th armies were in for a bitter clash with the major enemy force that was seeking to envelop them.

The situation was made worse because the 11th German Army, breaking through the defenses of the Southern Front, was striking out through Mogilev-Podolsky to outrank and envelop these three armies.

The troops of the Southwestern Front, acting in cooperation with the Southern Front, mounted counterattacks to hold up the enemy advance. They inflicted great losses on the enemy, but failed to stop him. The Germans regrouped partially and lashed out again at the withdrawing troops of the 6th and 12th armies. This time the two armies found themselves in a very grave situation indeed.

A considerable portion of the retreating units of these armies was surrounded. Lieutenant-General Muzychenko, the commander of the 6th Army, was wounded badly and taken prisoner. The same fate befell the commander of the 12th Army, General Ponedelin. Meanwhile, a very grave situation developed at this time on the Southern Fronts. Its 9th Army was fighting to escape encirclement.

The enemy's advance to the Dnieper and the breakthrough to Zaporozhye, Dnepropetrovsk, and Odessa gravely aggravated the situation of the Soviet troops along the entire Southwestern direction. However, the German forces had won this victory at great cost. They were badly exhausted and had sustained heavy losses.

2. The Battle of Moscow

Marshal of the Soviet Union Vasili Sokolovsky (1897–1968) served in the Soviet Army from 1918. During the Second World War, he was chief of staff of the Western Front and the commander of several fronts. After the war, he was a Deputy Minister of Defense, the Chief of the General Staff, and the Inspector General of the Ministry of Defense of the Soviet Union.

The events described below took place when General Sokolovsky was chief of staff of the Western Front.

In the first months of the war, following Nazi Germany's treacherous attack against the Soviet Union, we suffered defeats and setbacks.

There came wave after wave of German armies pushing on toward the east.

In late September, the German High Commander concentrated the largest grouping of its crack troops in the Moscow sector at the expense of other fronts. That grouping was supposed to capture Moscow by swift attack.

On the Moscow axis, we had three of our fronts—the Western, Reserve, and Bryansk—whose armies numbered a total of 800,000 officers and men. But whereas the difference was not big in numerical strength, the Germans had a considerable superiority over us in tanks and artillery: they had 1,700 tanks and 19,450 guns and mortars against our 770 tanks and 9,150 guns and mortars.

The Commander-in-Chief of the Western Front was General of the Army Georgi Zhukov, and I was the chief of staff.

The enemy's operation, code-named Typhoon, began on September 30 with an attack against the troops of the Bryansk Front, and on October 2 an attack was launched against the Western and Reserve fronts. The Germans broke through our defenses and advanced rapidly toward Vyazma.

The enemy's troops managed to penetrate deeply into the central regions of our country and reached the approaches to the capital. We had lost a vast area: thousands of villages, major railway junctions, and cities like Bryansk, Vyazma, Orel, Rzhev, Kalinin, and Sukhinichi.

On October 14 the German Command announced that the main Red Army forces had been encircled on the central Moscow axis. It said that 350,000 Soviet POWs and a large quantity of weapons had been captured, and 45 Soviet divisions encircled.

In actual fact, our 19th, 20th, 24th, and 32nd armies had been encircled in the Bryansk and Vyazma areas, or fewer than 20 divisions, many of them numbering only 2,000 to 3,000 servicemen each as a result of heavy losses in previous battles. Most of the troops of the Bryansk, Western, and Reserve fronts had withdrawn in an orderly manner by October 20 and established a new defensive front. The encircled Soviet troops held in position a considerable number of Nazi divisions. Later on, some of the troops broke out of the encirclement, and many units joined guerrilla detachments or formed new ones.

The battles on the Moscow axis cost the enemy dearly, too. According to German generals who had taken part in the battles, they were stunned by the resistance put up by the Soviet troops and by their own tremendous losses on the approaches to Moscow.

General von Klüge, who commanded the Fourth Army, suggested to the Command of the Army Group Center that the offensive against Moscow be postponed until the spring of 1942 because of his army's big losses. The question of resuming the offensive against Moscow was discussed at a conference of commanders of army groups in Orsha. Commander of the Army Group South, General Field Marshal von Rundstedt, agreed with von Klüge and asked Commander-in-Chief of the Land Forces von Brauchitsch for reinforcements for his group for developing success on the Rostov axis. The commander of the reserve army, General Fromm, thought that a peaceful proposal should be made to the Soviet Union in order to avoid the risk of fighting on two fronts.

The High Command of the Land Forces and Field Marshal von Bock, the Commander of the Army Group Center, did not accept the generals' arguments. The fact that the Army Group Center was already at the outskirts of Moscow and that there had been successful operations of Nazi troops on the Tikhvin and Rostov axes had raised hopes for the capture of Moscow and a quick end to the war.

The Nazi High Command threw its best troops against Moscow. The Army Group Center had a considerable superiority over our forces putting up a defense on the Moscow axis. The Nazis had twice as many officers and men, two-and-a-half times as many guns and mortars, and one-and-a-half times as many tanks as our troops. On the flanks of the Western Front, where the Germans were delivering major blows with their tank armies (groups), they had an even greater superiority in manpower and materiel. The enemy also had a considerable superiority in bombers.

According to the plans of the German High Command, the 4th Field Army, jointly with Panzer armies (groups),

was to defeat the Soviet troops near Moscow and encircle
Moscow from the north and south. Moscow was to be
destroyed by artillery and aircraft, while the population
that would survive was to be destroyed by Sonderkommando
Moskau.

In assessing the situation on the Moscow axis in late
October, the Soviet Supreme command decided that although the enemy was weakened, he had sufficient forces
for resuming the offensive, whereas the Red Army did not
then have the capability of taking the offensive. That was
why the Soviet Command's main efforts were directed
toward the strengthening of the Western Front.

The General Headquarters reinforced the troops of the
Western Front with several fresh infantry, cavalry, and
tank divisions and brigades. The field units of the front
were being replenished with manpower and materiel. Most
of the armies of the front were reinforced with antitank
artillery and guards mortar units. All in all, the Western
Front received reinforcements totaling 100,000 officers
and men, 300 tanks, and 2,000 artillery pieces in the first
half of November. The other fronts operating on the Moscow axis were also reinforced.

The organization of defense of the Moscow outskirts
was carried out with the utmost strain. The armies in the
field had a considerable shortfall in numbers. There was
still a lack of armaments and ammunition. The troops were
in great need of motor vehicles, tractors, and even horses.
The flanks of the fronts where the enemy was making
preparations for the main blows remained unstable.

The enemy resumed the offensive near Moscow on November 15 and 16. Especially fierce fighting began in the
right wing of the front in the sector of the 30th and 16th
armies.

As a result of the stubborn resistance of Soviet troops,
the enemy's offensive northwest of Moscow was virtually
halted in late November: his pace of offensive in the last
week of November was only a half-mile to a mile a day.

On November 30 the Germans assumed the defensive on the front of the 30th Army commanded by General Lelyushenko, indicating that the enemy had abandoned his original plan to encircle Moscow from the east.

In the left wing of the front, the enemy resumed the offensive on November 18, delivering the main blow northeast of Tula in the direction of Venev-Kashira. On the first day of the offensive, with his superiority in forces, the enemy was able to break through the defenses of the 50th Army commanded by General Boldin and capture a number of important positions. The breakthrough of the defenses of the 50th Army east of Tula, coupled with the enemy's offensive west of Tula, posed the threat of encircling the city and made it necessary to take urgent measures for the defense of the entire left wing of the front.

To drive the enemy back where he had broken through in the sector of the 50th Army and to protect the Kashira axis, the Venev combat area where the left-flank units of the 50th Army had been withdrawn was established by an order of the front. In addition, the Ryazan, Zaraisk, Kashira, and Laptevo combat areas were established. The organization of defense by means of combat areas in the absence of a continuous front line was advisable in many cases. It was the system of combat areas that enabled the command of the front to restore the position of the 50th Army northeast of Tula in a difficult situation and to prepare conditions for the defeat of the enemy.

In view of the enemy's breakthrough into the Kashira area, the commander of the Western Front sent the 3rd Cavalry Corps commanded by General Belov to deploy southward from the area of Kashira, rout the enemy, and throw him back to the south. This task was accomplished successfully.

Fearing for his right flank, on November 30 Guderian (one of the Nazi commanders) ordered the 33rd Army Corps and the 10th Motorized Division of the 47th Panzer Corps to assume the defensive. The enemy's 17th Panzer

Division and the 29th Motorized Division received orders to repulse the attacks of General Belov's mobile grouping and consolidate their positions on the line north of Mordves. Thus, already by November 30, Guderian in fact admitted that it was impossible to carry out the task set though he tried to make the operations of the 24th Panzer Corps more active north of Tula. The 24th Panzer Corps failed in its attempts to reach the Moscow-Tula highway and sustained heavy losses.

The German Command, which had lost its sense of reality, could no longer appraise the situation soberly. Despite the obvious failure of the offensive northwest and southwest of Moscow, the Command of the Army Group Center made a desperate attempt to break through to Moscow from the northwest and west and complete the encirclement of our troops in the area of Tula. The offensive was to begin simultaneously in all directions, without a lull or regrouping of the troops.

North of Moscow, General Reinhardt tried to break through to Moscow from the direction of Krasnaya Polyana and Kryukovo, committing a fresh tank division to action. General Hoeppner tried to deal a blow in the direction of Nakhabino and encircle the 5th Army and enter Moscow from the west, jointly with the 4th Army which was attacking from the area of Naro-Fominsk in the direction of Golitsino.

On December 1 the enemy succeeded in pushing back our troops and made considerable advance in the Krasnaya Polyana and Naro-Fominsk axes, where he captured several strongpoints of our troops. The commanders of the 20th, 5th, and 33rd armies of the Western Front were assigned the task of repelling the enemy's blows. On December 2 the advance units of the 20th Army beat off all the enemy's attacks and forced him to stop his offensive. The enemy's attacks in the sector of the 16th Army commanded by General Rokossovsky were also repulsed.

From December 3 to December 5, the 1st Shock Army

and the 20th Army dealt several strong blows on the enemy, dislodging him from a number of important inhabited localities. On the same days, the 16th Army repelled several of the enemy's fierce attacks in the area of Kryukovo. The left-flank divisions of the 16th Army, together with the 5th Army, threw the enemy back from a major bend of the Moskva River and liberated several inhabited localities northeast of Zvenigorod. To rout the enemy's troops which had broken through, General Yefremov, commander of the 33rd Army, formed a shock group under whose attacks the enemy retreated from Yushkovo and Burtsevo on December 4 and began to withdraw to the line of the Nara River. The enemy troops that had penetrated into the sector of the 5th Army were also destroyed.

Thus, from December 1 to December 5, the troops of the right wing and the center of the Western Front inflicted the first defeat on the enemy with powerful counterblows and seized the initiative. As a result, in early December, the enemy's last attempts to break through to Moscow were frustrated in the center and flanks of the Western Front and he was actually forced to assume the defensive on the entire Moscow axis.

The idea of launching a counteroffensive near Moscow was considered in early November, when the enemy's tank armies were stopped on the near approaches to Moscow. At that time, the General Headquarters of the Supreme Command issued an order to concentrate four reserve armies which were to be attached to the fronts of the western axis for a counteroffensive in the Moscow area.

For this counteroffensive, the Supreme Command decided to commit the troops of three fronts: the Kalinin and Western fronts and the right flank of the Southwestern Front. The main efforts were to be concentrated in the zone of the Western Front, which had the task of routing the enemy's shock Panzer groupings advancing toward Moscow. To capitalize on surprise, the counteroffensive was to begin immediately, almost by the same grouping of troops that had been formed during the defensive battle.

In its first counteroffensive, the Red Army had no decisive superiority over the enemy in its forces and had fewer artillery pieces. It was only in aircraft—including the planes of the antiaircraft defense force and the Moscow zone, as well as obsolete models—that the Red Army had a two-to-one superiority on the Western axis.

If one is to speak about the advantages of the Red Army in that period they consisted, above all, in its moral and political superiority over the Nazi troops, confidence in the rightness of its cause, and unshakable will for victory. This was the decisive factor which made the Nazi invader retreat from Moscow.

The surprise blow of the Soviet troops northwest and southwest of Moscow stunned the Nazi Command.

As a result of sharp deterioration of the situation near Moscow, on December 8 Hitler signed a directive to assume the defensive on the entire Soviet-German front. The German High Command hoped that it would be able to repel the Red Army's counteroffensive and replenish its troops with men and materiel.

The troops of the Kalinin, Western, and Southwestern fronts carried on the counteroffensive unceasingly. To keep up the momentum of the offensive, new mobile groups were formed of tank, cavalry, and infantry units.

As a result of the counteroffensive, the main forces of the enemy's 3rd and 4th Panzer armies were routed. The threat to Moscow from the northwest was averted. Over 500 villages and towns of the Moscow Region were liberated. The Kalinin-Moscow railway was thus cleared of enemy troops.

The offensive of the Western Front in the area of Tula and the right wing of the Southwestern Front in the area of Yelets was developing successfully at the same time as the counteroffensive northwest of Moscow.

The crossing of the Oka River on the Kaluga-Belev

sector provided favorable conditions for encircling the main forces of the Army Group Center from the southwest. However, the Soviet troops on the offensive were strained to the utmost. The logistics units did not have time to supply the troops on the offensive with ammunition. And, at that time, the Western Front had no possibilities of forming a new grouping of troops for dealing a blow in the direction of Vyazma and linking up with the forces of the Kalinin Front.

The counteroffensive in the center of the Western Front in late December was successful. After breaking through the enemy's defenses on the Nara River, the units of the 33rd Army commanded by General Yefremov liberated the town of Naro-Fominsk on December 26. Maloyaroslavets was liberated on January 2, and Borovsk on January 4, 1942.

Upset by the breakthrough of our troops deep into the rear of its own troops, the Nazi Command urgently brought up to the area of Vyazma new units from other sectors of the front which, together with the air force, repelled the attacks of our troops on Vyazma from the north and south. At the same time, the enemy struck powerful counter-blows on the lines of communication of the 33rd and 29th armies, which had moved forward so that their units had to assume the defensive under unfavorable conditions. In early February, when it seemed that the Army Group Center was doomed, the enemy managed to halt the advance of the Western and Kalinin fronts. The offensive of the Bryansk Front also failed.

Thus, due to losses and lack of reserves, the offensive potential of the three fronts of the western axis was virtually exhausted. We had failed to complete the rout of the Army Group Center. The troops of the three fronts operating on the western axis gradually had to assume the defensive.

On the whole, however, despite their inconclusiveness, the offensive operations of the Red Army on the western axis in January–March 1942 were crowned with new victories. The enemy was repulsed another 50 to 60 miles in the sector of the Western Front and 100 to 250 miles altogether, and in the sector of the Kalinin Front, another 100 to 150 miles.

The units of the Western and Kalinin fronts and of the right wing of the Southwestern Front inflicted a major defeat on crack Nazi troops. Near Moscow 38 German divisions were routed, including 11 Panzer, 4 motorized, and 23 infantry divisions. The rest of the divisions of the Army Group Center were bled white. Three out of four German Panzer armies operating on the Soviet-German front were routed. The fields near Moscow were covered with German weapons and military equipment. All in all, in the Battle of Moscow, the Nazis lost about 500,000 officers and men—the pick of the Wehrmacht. Six armies of the Army Group Center lost about 80 percent of their artillery pieces, tanks, vehicles, and other materiel.

The defeat of the Nazi troops near Moscow was of tremendous political and strategic importance. Hitler's plan of blitzkrieg against the Soviet Union had failed completely. The German army had lost its strategic initiative and was forced to assume the defensive for the first time since the war started two-and-a-half years earlier. Instead of the expected quick victory, Nazi Germany was faced with a protracted war.

The victory near Moscow marked the beginning of a new stage in the liberation movement of the European nations against their Nazi oppressors. Whereas, in 1941, in most European countries the liberation movement consisted of isolated guerrilla detachments and groups of patriots carrying out separate operations, after the Battle of Moscow this movement began to acquire a nationwide character.

The Red Army's victory in the Battle of Moscow also had a considerable effect on the final formation of an antifascist coalition. On January 1, 1942, a declaration was signed by twenty-six countries which pledged to mobilize all their resources for the struggle against the aggressors and not to conclude a separate peace treaty with them. Somewhat later, an Anglo-Soviet treaty on the alliance against Nazi Germany and a Soviet-American agreement on the principles applying to mutual aid in the prosecution of the war against aggression were signed. The antifascist coalition played an important role in the victory over Nazi Germany.

3. Battle of Stalingrad

Marshal of the Soviet Union Andrei Yeremenko (1892–1970) served in the armed forces since 1913. During World War II he commanded the armies and troops of a number of fronts. After the war, he commanded a number of military districts and was Inspector General of the USSR Ministry of Defense.

During the events described below, he commanded the Stalingrad Front.

In August and September 1942, the most difficult period of the defense of Stalingrad—the preparation for a counteroffensive—began.

In areas just north and south of Stalingrad, we set up good starting points for a counteroffensive.

In September 1942, the question of a counteroffensive was raised in a conversation with the Supreme Commander, Stalin. I understood that a plan for a counteroffensive was also being worked out at General Headquarters.

After talking to the Supreme Commander as usual, I shared my views about the counteroffensive with my chief of staff. As we talked, we came to the conclusion that the

Nazi troops at Stalingrad were on the verge of a serious crisis. They had suffered severe and irreparable losses, and all their attempts to build up reserves had come to nothing. All the plans for capturing the city had failed completely, and the dates earmarked for its capture came and went.

The time had come to strike the enemy at his most vulnerable places—in the northern and southern flanks—without letting up resistance in the city itself.

As a result of our conversation, we had come to certain conclusions. We put them down on paper and sent them to GHQ. The substance of the resulting document: "The enemy near Stalingrad could be defeated by blows delivered by powerful groupings from the north in the direction of Kalach and from the south from the positions of the 57th and 51st armies in the direction of Abganerovo and further on toward the northwest [also in the direction of Kalach].''

Thus we briefly formulated the strategy that had been born a long time ago of two converging blows from the middle reaches of the Don and from the area south of Stalingrad. This strategy was to be put into effect by the combined operations of the Stalingrad and Don Fronts.

We knew the German generals who commanded the troops at Stalingrad very well both from intelligence data and personal experience gained in combat operations. No doubt General Paulus (who was later given the rank of General Field Marshal) and his chief of staff General Schmidt were experienced military leaders. They had been assigned an impossible task, but they displayed much resourcefulness in carrying it out.

There was no denying that General Hoth who commanded the 4th Panzer Army was experienced and assertive. Von Richthofen, commander of the 4th Air Force, was noted for his Nazi fanaticism.

Of course, we also knew of some commanders in the lower ranks—corps and division commanders like General Fromeri, the commander of the 29th Panzer Division, who was a rather young but sufficiently experienced and resolute officer, and General Pfeffer, commander of the 297th Infantry Division, who was extremely ambitious and ready to take action regardless of the losses that might result.

In early October, General Vasilevsky, chief of the General Staff, arrived at our front and said that our outline of the plan had been approved by GHQ and that the counteroffensive was planned for the second week of November. He told us about the forces and equipment assigned to the front for the operation, and we exchanged views on the forthcoming action.

On several days before the counteroffensive, the weather was cloudy and foggy, a great help in concentrating our troops in assault positions.

Three days before the counteroffensive, I was informed of GHQ's decision to commence the operations of the Stalingrad Front 24 hours later than those of the other two fronts. This decision partly satisfied my request to delay the operations by 48 hours.

Such a delay could bring us greater success with less effort. We had to make the enemy believe that the breakthrough in the north was the only danger facing him, and therefore we had to make him throw all his reserves—particularly his tank reserves—only at this point. Since the enemy's reserves were small and based near Stalingrad, his forces in the zone of our planned advance would be weakened by the Nazi Command's transferring its troops from areas it considered safe. They would be removed from prepared positions and begin concentration in order to nullify our offensive in the north. This would be the moment when we would strike unexpectedly from the south.

The day of November 19 was drawing to a close. We had a long night of waiting ahead of us.

I was absolutely confident that the operation would be successful, but still I was worried. A large number of motor vehicles had remained on the left bank due to an increasing amount of floating ice in the Volga, and the fuel tanks of the vehicles that had been moved across the river were only half-full. But I was worried mostly for the reason every army commander worries before a battle: the lives of thousands of people are in his hands. To achieve victory without causing his compatriots needless casualties and bloodshed—could such a task be accomplished without worry? Indeed, the commander of a front cannot help worrying before an offensive, but he must not show his feelings to those around him.

At night, I made another check on our preparedness and was informed that everything was ready for battle and that the troops had finished their last preparations and taken up assault positions. The artillery was in its fire positions. To keep our intentions secret, the artillery had made range adjustments by firing single guns of different caliber at different times; mechanized units were carefully camouflaged, and after dark they moved into starting positions.

The units of the German 29th Motorized Division of the 4th Panzer Army and the Romanian 6th Army Corps of the Romanian 4th Army were in the zone of attack of the strike force of the Stalingrad Front.

I could hardly sleep that night. I got up about 6:00 A.M. and went out. The sky was growing pale in the east. Dawn was approaching, and a thin fog was floating over the ground.

We wanted to start operations on time—at 8:00 A.M. —and hoped that the fog would not be dense. With my permission, the chief of staff phoned the army commanders and gave them the signal for beginning the artillery preparation at the appointed hour.

By 7:00 A.M., I was already at the forward observation post of the 57th Army, from which the entire sector of the main attack could be clearly visible. Unfortunately, the fog prevented a clear view. General Tolbukhin, who commanded the army, was not at the observation post; he was obviously elsewhere, with some other division. But I had the army chief of artillery Chistyakov with me.

The fog got thicker and the level of visibility dropped further—it was not more than 225 yards; the artillerymen were worried. And now heavy snow began to fall. It was inevitable that the commanders of the 51st and 57th armies would request that the commencement of the artillery preparation be postponed by one hour, and I agreed to their request. Then I delayed it by another hour. The Supreme Command was nervous and constantly demanding that we begin the offensive at once. I even got angry with the officers at GHQ and told them that I was not sitting in an office, but was at the battlefield and would know when to begin.

Then it was 9:00 A.M. Officers and men were on edge as they waited for the signal. The infantrymen were ready for assault, the artillerymen had loaded their guns, and all the crews had taken their stations. The rumbling of tank motors being warmed up could be heard in the distance.

The fog had lifted enough and visibility and become almost normal. At 9:30 A.M. I have the signal to begin at 10:00. The rocket launchers opened up and were followed by guns and mortars.

Several minutes before the infantry and tanks launched their offensive, we threw all our weapons into the attack: mortars, machine guns, submachine guns, and rifles. Powerful mortars fired almost at the moment of the attack. Endless waves of our soldiers rose from the trenches with cries of "Hurrah!" and the rumbling of the tank motors was heard.

The offensive did not start simultaneously because of the fog and insufficient numbers of artillery which consecutively pounded enemy positions before one attacking army, then another. However, the operation was a complete success. The enemy's forward line of defense, which had been fortified heavily, was broken through.

I should like to dwell for a moment on an instructive example which occurred on November 20 in the breakthrough zone of General Tolbukhin's army. As I have already said, the artillery preparation was started by the rocket launchers. They were to make two strikes: the first one indicated the beginning of the artillery preparation, and the second one (at the end of the artillery preparation) signaled the start of the attack by the infantry and tanks. When problems of control, cooperation, and signals were being settled, it seemed that this system was clear to everyone; but it turned out to be otherwise. We were watching the start of battle operations from our observation post: the rocket launchers began pounding the enemy's positions. I looked through my binoculars from right to left and saw that on the left flank our infantry had risen into the attack and was approaching the enemy's forward trenches. This made me break into a cold sweat. Once the attack began, it was impossible to stop it.

Instead of committing the 143rd Marine Brigade to attack after the second strike launched by the rocket launchers, its commander did so after the first strike. What was to be done? Artillery preparation would have to be cut short. It was just as well that this had happened not in the direction of the main blow, but on its flank. I called Tolbukhin, who was at a divisional command post on the right flank, and asked him whether he knew that the 143rd Brigade had begun the attack without an artillery preparation and what he intended doing about it. He replied that he did not know and for the moment was at a loss. I then decided that the bombardment should be stopped in that sector and artillery support provided for the infantry. This was done, and the attack was successful. Within the space of twenty minutes, the brigade crossed the second line of trenches and began to disappear beyond the horizon. The courageous 143rd Brigade was given full backup, including armored support.

The artillery bombardment was not yet over when two brigades had entered the breakthrough and were followed by the 13th Mechanized Corps which was intended for developing the attack.

So it sometimes happens in wartime that an unforeseen incident may not only prevent the situation from deteriorating, but on the contrary improve it, so long as one keeps calm and does not hesitate to change original plans.

By the evening of November 22, the troops of the Stalingrad Front had carried out their part of the task to surround the enemy at Stalingrad. By that time, both the major routes which connected the enemy with his rear had been cut: Kotelnikovo-Stalingrad and Kalach-Stalingrad.

That same evening, Stalin phoned me and asked if it was true that we had captured the station of Krivomuzginskaya. I said yes.

"Excellent! Tomorrow you must link up with the Southwestern Front, whose troops have reached Kalach."

"Yes, sir," I replied.

The next day, November 23, the troops of the two fronts linked up between Krivomuzginskaya and Kalach. Twenty-two enemy divisions had found themselves in a rather tight ring. The operational encirclement had been completed.

As a result of the offensive, the front had achieved its assigned objective. The Romanian 6th Army Corps had been routed, and its 1st, 2nd, and 18th infantry divisions no longer existed; the 29th mechanized division had sustained heavy losses; 10,000 officers and men were taken prisoner, and a large amount of equipment was seized.

During the counteroffensive the soldiers of the Stalingrad Front displayed unparalleled courage. Here is one example:

Private Popov, grenades at the ready, was with his platoon as it ran to attack the enemy. Some twenty steps away, three German soldiers were running from him. Suddenly they took refuge in a trench. Popov threw a grenade and killed two of them, but the third, firing back, jumped out of the trench, wounding Popov in his left arm. Popov threw a second grenade. The German was killed instantly. A medical orderly ran up to Popov and offered to bandage his left arm and send him to the hospital. But Popov said,

"No, I can't go to the hospital—I have to go to that house over there. We've got to take it."

And again he was running, flinging himself down, crawling, throwing grenades and firing. He was wounded two more times. When he was wounded again, he lost consciousness for a while. When he came to, he asked the orderly, who bent over him, "Where are we?"

"In the house which we were ordered to capture."

"Well, now you can take me to the hospital," said Popov like a man who had just finished some urgent business.

The swift offensive resulted in the linkup between the troops of the Stalingrad Front of those of the Southwestern Front. The steel ring of encirclement was complete. Thus the Stalingrad Front, which bore the brunt of the enemy's incessant offensive blows, not only held out, inflicting heavy losses on the enemy, but pierced the enemy lines and routed the German troops in the ensuing counteroffensive.

During the same period, the troops of the two neighboring fronts accomplished a great deal as well. The strike group of the Southwestern Front fulfilled its mission. Having reached the Don River in the Kalach sector, it cut off the enemy's lines of retreat to the southwest and west, and, in cooperation with our front, completed the ring of encirclement.

At the Don Front our situation was somewhat less favorable. Despite three days of heavy fighting, the strike group of the 24th Army could not break through the enemy defenses and separate the enemy's Trans-don and Stalingrad groupings. The enemy still held on to the river crossings. So, at that time, the troops of our front failed to surround the enemy completely. The offensive of all the three fronts, which intended to scatter the surrounded enemy troops, began on December 4. Heavy fighting went on for five days, but no appreciable results were achieved because the enemy had managed to organize his defenses at new, advantageous positions, setting up an efficient system of fire. At the same time, the enemy had managed to ascertain the direction of our main blow. To prevent its success, the Nazi Command had brought in the most reliable and fully manned formations from other directions. It should be borne in mind that the bulk of our artillery had not been brought up by the beginning of the offensive and that our soldiers were very tired after the previous ten days of incessant battles.

Our offensive was stopped. We realized that it was impossible to break up and destroy the encircled enemy troops quickly. It was necessary to reinforce our armies' offensive with fresh forces.

At that time we faced great difficulties in supplying the troops with munitions, fuel, and rations because the drifting ice floes in the Volga had become an insurmountable obstacle both for ferries and launches. We had to use what supplies we had very sparingly.

However, the enemy's supplies were even scarcer because we had taken resolute measures against his supply air routes. It was a genuine air blockade established by our fighter planes in close cooperation with antiaircraft artillery.

By the beginning of December, the encircled enemy troops were on the verge of catastrophe because of their complete lack of transport communication with the outside world. However, their plight did not persuade either the Nazi High Command or the commanders of the encircled German units to make a sober appraisal of the situation and of the real correlation of forces. They still hoped to retain the Stalingrad bridgehead occupied by the 6th and 4th armies (which were later combined) and to reestablish communications with them through simultaneous strikes from outside and from within against one of the sections of the ring formed by our troops.

The German Command made every effort to free its troops from the encirclement. First it attempted to deliver counterblows from the area of Kotelnikovo. With a view to reconnoitering the actual forces of that grouping, the

Command of the Stalingrad Front decided to deliver a strike at Kotelnikovo on December 1 with a cavalry corps supported by a tank brigade. After three days of fierce fighting, these troops were beaten off from Kotelnikovo, with heavy losses, by enemy armored units (about 200 tanks of the German 57th Panzer Corps). But they accomplished their primary mission and the enemy's intentions were discovered. It was not clear where his main grouping had been concentrated.

The battle between the Soviet troops and the units of the German Fourth Panzer Army continued unabated for twelve days. Because of great losses, the enemy's thrust had somewhat weakened by December 23. But our troops had also sustained considerable losses.

Taking into account the need for decisive action, the command of the front informed GHQ of its plan to rout the Kotelnikovo enemy grouping. This plan envisaged striking the main blow by the right flank at Kotelnikovo along the Don River. The blow was to be dealt partly against the enemy's flank; it could be delivered quickly and did not require any maneuver or regrouping of manpower and materiel. GHQ gave its approval. Its implementation ensured that we would be successful in routing the enemy's Kotelnikovo grouping. After the plan had been carried out, the encircled German troops would lose any hope of being relieved.

The 235th Tank Brigade and the 21st Antitank Brigade distinguished themselves in those battles. These units, which fought to the last shell and to the last cartridge, did not yield one inch of ground to the enemy. In those battles they lost almost all their weapons and equipment, which were either damaged or destroyed. For example, the 21st Brigade lost all of its 60 guns, but it delayed the enemy's advance, made him suffer great losses, and gained nearly a week of precious time, which actually saved the situation. It was only on December 19 that the enemy, who had brought up another Panzer division and the Viking Motorized Division, could advance a little farther. But in those six days of fighting the advance units of General Malinovsky's army had arrived.

By December 30, the counterblow by the troops of the Stalingrad Front at Manstein's grouping had been carried out successfully: the enemy had been routed and the operational situation of our troops had improved radically.

As a result, the intention of the Nazi Command to break through the ring of our troops and relieve the German armies encircled at Stalingrad failed miserably. The remnants of the routed troops from Hoth-Manstein's strike grouping scattered to the southwest and the west.

Soon afterward, the Stalingrad Front was designated the Southern Front and was assigned the mission of advancing on Rostov.

The Don Front, which had received the main armies of the Stalingrad Front and which was commanded by General Rokossovsky, was assigned the mission of eliminating the encircled German troops.

The plan of this mission was to break up the encircled German troops and destroy them piecemeal.

Operations to put the plan into effect began on January 10, 1943, after the Command of the German 6th Army refused to accept an ultimatum to surrender.

In the first three days of the offensive, our troops advanced 5 to 6 miles and the western salient of the encircled troops was destroyed, but we could not split the enemy's grouping. The enemy decided to let the noose tighten further, but prevented us from splitting up his forces.

By the evening of January 17, our troops advanced 12 to 15 miles and approached the enemy's outer ring of defenses. However, we again failed to split the encircled enemy grouping. But the area held by this grouping had been almost halved. In the next three days, the troops of our front were getting ready to break through the defenses of the encircled German troops which had been set up at the inner ring. On January 22, the offensive was resumed and the enemy defenses were penetrated.

On January 26, the 21st Army linked up with the 62nd Army in the area of Mamayev Kurgan, and the encircled enemy grouping was finally split up.

On January 25, 1943, entire German units began to surrender. By January 31, the southern group of the encircled enemy troops ceased to resist and surrendered. On the same day, General Field Marshal Paulus was taken prisoner.

The Battle of Stalingrad was a decisive battle in the defeat of Nazi Germany; it signified a turning point in the course of the Second World War. Stalin was right when he said that Stalingrad meant the decline of the German army. "After Stalingrad," he said, "the Germans could never recover."

4. Breaking the Siege of Leningrad

Marshal of the Soviet Union Kirill Meretskov (1897–1968) served in the army from 1916. During the Second World War he was the commander of an army and later of various fronts. After the war he was the commander of several military districts and a Deputy Minister of Defense. At the time of the breaking of the Leningrad blockade, he commanded the Volkhov Front.

On October 6, 1942, the Sinyavino operation by the Volkhov Front which I commanded ended in failure. But although the blockade of Leningrad was not broken in the course of the operation, conditions had been created for launching a powerful winter offensive whose aim would be to establish a safe corridor between beleaguered Leningrad and the rest of the country. This mission was to be accomplished by the troops of the Leningrad and Volkhov fronts. When Marshal of the Soviet Union Voroshilov and General of the Army Zhukov, who were in charge of coordination of their operations, arrived at the front, they made a detailed study of the situation. We discussed the forthcoming operation, which could succeed if the actions of the Leningrad and Volkhov fronts were coordinated closely. It was therefore necessary for me to see General Govorov, who commanded the Leningrad Front. In view of the difficult situation in Leningrad, it was decided that Govorov should remain in Leningrad and I should meet him there. Having received the permission of the Supreme Command General Headquarters, I set off at once.

It was late October. I looked intently at the familiar Leningrad streets which were so dear to me. They used to be filled with people, but now they were empty and looked lifeless. I felt a lump in my throat.

"What part can you take in the forthcoming operation?" I asked Govorov.

"We can deliver an encounter attack, but only in the area where your troops are close to Leningrad. We do not have enough forces for a deep-going operation," he replied.

It was clear that we would have to break the blockage somewhere near Lake Ladoga. This posed extremely difficult tasks for my front, especially since it was there, in the area of Schlisselburg and Sinyavino, that the battles had just ended which had failed to bring the desired result.

The plan which we worked out provided for a joint strike to be carried out by the Leningrad and Volkhov fronts from opposite directions to defeat the enemy grouping south of Ladoga and break the blockade at the narrowest place, with the participation of a greater number of divisions of the Volkhov Front. This plan was submitted to the Supreme Command General Headquarters and approved about a month later. Preparations were to last throughout December. I was to meet Govorov again in early January in order to discuss details of our joint attack. Meanwhile munitions and new materiel were being supplied to our fronts. In the preparations for the operation, the "Road of Life" across icebound Lake Ladoga once again played a great role. In mid-December, when Lake Ladoga became frozen over, supply trucks started moving in long columns across the islands of the lake.

Somewhat earlier, foreseeing that this route would again be used, the Nazis made an attempt to cut it, but were defeated at Sukho Island. The ice route began operating again without hindrance, with the exception of intensive bombings by the Luftwaffe.

On December 8 the order came from the Supreme Command General Headquarters to break the blockade. The operation for breaking the blockade was code-named Iskra (Spark).

In studying the map, I noted again and again with distress how strongly the enemy had fortified the sector between Lipki and Mishkino, where its 18th Army was stationed. The sector was a powerful fortified area with a ramified system of antipersonnel and antitank obstacles, continuous minefields, and additional engineer installations along deep ditches in peat bogs. It was hard for our tanks and heavy artillery to gain access. The enemy's defense line consisted of five centers of resistance with many artillery and machine-gun emplacements, trenches and minefields, dense barbed-wire entanglements, and two fairly high ice-covered ramparts. This was the sector which the troops of the Volkhov Front were to attack.

We began forming a shock group. Its core was the 2nd Shock Army commanded by Lieutenant-General Romanovsky. We transferred to it a considerable quantity of artillery from other armies, the reserve of the front, and everything that the Supreme Command General Headquarters could give us. The density of the German troops at this sector was almost double that provided for by their field manuals. But we were also able to concentrate on average 250 guns and mortars per mile, which made it possible to have an extremely high density of fire.

The planned artillery offensive was given special attention. In addition, at preliminary meetings and then in the course of special exercises, we rehearsed a harmonious combination of an artillery attack with air support. For this purpose, almost the entire front air force, consisting of the

14th Air Army commanded by Major-General Zhuravlev, was redirected to the right flank of the front.

It would have been a waste of forces to attack the enemy's centers of resistance head-on. But, because of the specific features of the terrain, neither was it possible to bypass them. My Chief of Staff General Sharokhin and his officers had to study the enemy positions very carefully in order to organize the offensive with maximum effectiveness and to minimize our losses.

Such is war. When a commander plans an operation, he not only realizes that there will be losses in manpower, but he also roughly foresees inevitable losses since he does not want to miscalculate and cause still heavier losses as a result of underestimation of several factors. This is one of the features of the military profession. To save millions, we throw into action tens of thousands of people while being aware that many thousands may die. This is military logic. Unfortunately, we have to take into account the inevitable loss of life. But all this still does not turn a military officer into some sort of a machine devoid of all feeling.

I have always taken any losses very close to heart. I must say this even if some people may regard this as a weakness.

Throughout December the troops were making intense preparations for the operation. Commanders were assembled and war games were held. The units were trained at camps built on the approximate model of the centers of defense which they would have to overcome later on. Aerial photography provided a wealth of information, and our military engineers quickly put up structures resembling the enemy ice rampart, pillboxes on the marsh, and various field fortifications. Commanders of formations worked out in detail questions relating to the cooperation of the fighting units. Several times I checked on their readiness for the operation. The Sinyavino operation had been a lesson for all of us.

In early January 1943, I had another meeting with General Govorov. We discussed in detail the future joint actions and agreed on the lines of rendezvous. It was decided that if the troops of one of the fronts should be unable to reach the specified line, the troops of the other front would not stop their advance but would continue advancing until linkup. We also agreed on a set of code signals in order to avoid errors upon rendezvous. We went over the methods of turning our divisions after their linkup to the south in order to prepare a strike through Sinyavino in the direction of the middle reaches of the Moika River, in accordance with the order of the Supreme Command General Headquarters. Govorov and I understood each other without difficulty.

Until January 11 the troops continued to occupy their previous positions. I forbade them even to get closer to the starting positions ahead of time, so that our offensive that was being prepared would not be detected by enemy reconnaissance. It was only on the night of January 11 that our troops took their starting positions. A day later, our 14th Air Army delivered a massive strike on the enemy's rear. Of course, the headquarters of the German 18th Army understood by then that we would attack, but it could not change anything in a few hours.

On January 12, at 9:30 A.M. tons of deadly metal were dropped on the Nazi positions. The air and artillery preparations were going on for about two hours, and then the Soviet divisions rushed forward. Almost at once we discovered the sector where the German resistance was the strongest: the Kruglaya Grove, which had caused us so much difficulty during the Sinyavino operation. Close combat was going on there the whole day, often turning into hand-to-hand fighting. The Nazis would not surrender and were firing to the last cartridge, but it did not change the course of the battle. In the evening, this center of resistance fell and the 327th Division, which was renamed the 64th Guards Division for its feat, launched an offensive against the concentration area of the 207th Division of the Nazis, bypassing their fortified area from the north.

On January 13 and 14 I ordered the second echelon to go into action. The 18th Rifle Division commanded by Major-General Ovchinnikov supported by the 98th Tank Brigade broke through to the Germans' fortified area. At the same time, the 136th Division of the Leningrad Front was approaching it from the west. The enemy's centers of resistance had been isolated and cut off. All attempts by the fresh German units brought in from Mga to break through to them failed. The day of January 14 was spent on consolidating our success. We had to make one more effort to reach Leningrad, a heroic city, which was stretching its hand to the troops of the Volkhov Front. Our fronts had to advance one last mile—the most difficult one—to break the blockade.

On January 15–17 the troops of the two fronts stubbornly fought on, creating a corridor as they were doing so, recapturing territory from the enemy yard by yard and at the same time widening the breaches in the Germans' defenses in the flanks. The advance was more difficult in the south. In the direction of the Moika River, our troops encountered ever-growing resistance and obstacles which were increasingly difficult to surmount. It was easier to advance northward because the Germans who were wedged in between Soviet divisions and Lake Ladoga could not receive reinforcements. They had been concentrated north of the centers of resistance to divide the battle formations of the 372nd Division and break through to Sinyavino. But the Soviet 12th Ski-and-Rifle Brigade rushed into the enemy rear across Lake Ladoga and cut off the enemy grouping's communication with its command. As a result, the situation for the Germans near Lipki became hopeless, and the troops of the 128th Division broke their resistance. Finally, the 64th Guards Division and the 376th Division broke through into the station of Sinyavino.

Is it worth recalling the names of such small localities as

Sinyavino, Lipki, Workers' Settlement No. 8? Yes, it is, for fierce battles were raging there for days on end, hundreds and even dozens of yards were being overcome with great efforts, and Soviet soldiers performed immortal feats. One of them covered a Nazi machine gun with his body, another exploded himself with a grenade, killing ten German soldiers, a third returned to his unit from a medical battalion before his wounds were healed, and a fourth crawled under fire to a village occupied by the Germans, took his position in a house, and beat off several attacks by a German unit until our reinforcements came. I leafed through our front newspapers and read about heroic deeds of our servicemen. But war correspondents could not record everything.

I must recall one incident. During our breakthrough of the enemy defenses the Nazi Command threw into action the new heavy Tiger tank, which had been tested previously at Stalingrad and was intended for storming Leningrad. This monster was stopped by our antitank riflemen who had damaged the observation devices of the tank. Its crew could not hold out and ran away, leaving behind the machine, which was almost intact. The Nazis were keeping it under continuous fire and even tried to get it back through counterattacks.

Later I ordered that the Tiger be taken to our proving ground, where we studied its armor and discovered its vulnerable spots. Our industry developed new and very powerful shells and 152-mm self-propelled guns so that in the summer of 1943, when the Nazis made massive attacks with their heavy tanks in the Battle of the Kursk Bulge, we were not caught unprepared.

January 18, 1943 was a day of great victory of our two fronts, as well as of the whole of the Red Army and all the Soviet people. The 18th German Army had additionally detailed one unit from each of its formations for the last line of intermediate defense passing through Workers' Settlements Nos. 1 and 5. But it was in vain. The 18th

Division of the Volkhov Front in the south and the 372nd
Division in the north, together with the heroic defenders of
Leningrad, broke the Nazi ring and freed the city from its
blockade.

5. The Tank Battle at Kursk

Chief Marshal of the Armored Forces Pavel Rotmistrov (1901–1982) volunteered for the army in 1919. During the Second World War he commanded a tank corps and later a tank army. After the war he was commander of the armored forces of a military district, Commander of the Armored Forces Academy, an assistant to the Minister of Defense, and Inspector General of the USSR Ministry of Defense.

In the Battle of the Kursk Bulge he commanded the 5th Guards Tank Army.

After the rout of the Nazi troops at Stalingrad, and following subsequent offensive operations in the winter of 1942–43, a considerable part of Soviet territory was liberated. Our troops recaptured areas to the north, west, and south of Kursk, and Kursk itself was liberated. The so-called Kursk Bulge, formed on a front of about 350 miles in the course of the winter and spring offensives of Soviet troops and penetrating deep into the positions of the Nazi armies, enabled Soviet troops to strike a blow at the flanks and rear of the enemy groupings concentrated in the areas of Orel and Belgorod.

The Nazi Command thought that the Kursk Bulge, extending far westward, provided favorable conditions for encirclement and subsequent defeat of the Soviet troops of the Central and Voronezh fronts, which were on the defensive there. It worked out a plan code-named Citadel.

For carrying out Operation Citadel, whose purpose was to encircle and destroy the Soviet grouping by sudden converging blows in the general direction of Kursk, the German Command concentrated 50 divisions north and south of Kursk (including 16 Panzer and motorized divisions) which totaled about 900,000 men. They had up to 10,000 guns and mortars, about 2,700 tanks and assault guns, and over 2,000 aircraft. Incidentally, the troops of Germany's satellites were not employed in the battle.

The Adolf Hitler, Totenkopf, and Reich SS Panzer and motorized divisions, among others, were poised in the direction of the main blow. They were armed with the latest tanks and Ferdinand self-propelled guns. Their operations were to be covered by the elite air force units of the German army. German industry, which had at its disposal the economic resources of almost the whole of Europe, was manufacturing armaments and military equipment which were to enable the Wehrmacht to take revenge for its defeat in Stalingrad and recapture its lost initiative. General Mellentin, the former chief of staff of the 48th German Panzer Corps, later admitted that no other offensive had been prepared so carefully as that one.

Only large forces armed with the latest weapons could effectively counter the enemy's plans in such conditions. By the summer of 1943, the Soviet industry had supplied the front-line units with sufficient amounts of up-to-date armaments. The enemy's Orel grouping was opposed by the Soviet Central Front, which comprised five combined-arms armies, a tank army, an air army, and two tank corps. The Belgorod-Kharkov grouping of the enemy was opposed by the troops of the Voronezh Front that included five combined-arms armies, a tank army, an air army, two tank corps, and an infantry corps. On the eve of the battle, these two fronts alone—the Central Front commanded by General of the Army Rokossovsky and the Voronezh Front commanded by General of the Army Vatutin—had over 1,300,000 men, up to 20,000 guns and mortars, about 3,600 tanks and self-propelled guns, and more than 2,800 planes. The troops of these two fronts and the local population had built eight defense lines up to 190 miles deep.

The defense lines stood our troops in good stead in beating off the German attacks. But more important is that by this time the Red Army had strong tank and mechanized formations, as well as powerful artillery and high-performance aircraft.

The Soviet military art had risen to a new, higher level. The combat skills of Soviet officers and men had improved.

The Reserve Front, which was later renamed the Steppe Front, was formed. It had combined the Supreme Command's reserves in the southwestern direction.

These and other measures that had been taken turned the Kursk Bulge into a fiery antitank, antiartillery, antiaircraft, and antipersonnel defense area. Large artillery groupings were formed, along with powerful striking tank groupings.

The Nazi troops attacked at 5:30 A.M. on July 5.

Five infantry and three Panzer divisions struck at the positions of the 13th Army and the flank units of the 43rd and 70th armies of the Central Front. On the first day of the battle, the enemy brought into action five infantry and eight Panzer divisions and one motorized division against the positions of the 6th Army commanded by General Chistyakov and the 7th Guards Army under General Shumilov. The striking force of the German troops was composed of crack Panzer divisions and the Gross Deutschland Motorized Division. The positions of Soviet troops came under massive bombings. The Nazi Command spared neither shells nor manpower. The enemy threw into action up to thirty or forty Panzers against ten of our tanks.

The battle was growing more fierce. The Soviet soldiers were fighting to the last everywhere.

The plans of the Nazi Command to break through our defenses from marching columns were frustrated. Suffering heavy losses—the battlefield littered with burnt and damaged vehicles and equipment and with bodies of German officers and soldiers killed—the enemy was able to advance only 4 to 8 miles in some sectors.

But several crack Nazi Panzer divisions managed to break through to a depth of 20 miles. Two counterblows were delivered at the armored wedge of the enemy grouping which tried to widen the breach.

The defense lines of the 6th Guards Army and the 1st Tank Army proved to be insurmountable for the enemy. The German troops could not cut through our defenses and secure freedom to maneuver toward Oboyan.

Having failed to achieve the desired result in the direction of Oboyan, the Nazi Command decided to deliver the main blow against Prokhorovka and link up with its Orel grouping. The enemy concentrated four Panzer divisions and one infantry division in a narrow sector of the front, 5 to 6 miles wide, which meant that there were almost 160 Panzers and self-propelled guns for every mile. Up to 700 German fighting machines were waiting for the signal to attack Prokhorovka.

At the end of the day, on July 6, the 5th Guards Tank Army which I commanded received an order to advance 190 miles by forced march in three days and to assemble at Prokhorovka.

The combat situation brooked no delay. Having advanced the 190 miles, dust-covered machines with their crews hid in groves and copses. The technical condition of the vehicles was being checked.

Even now, several decades later, I can see those country roads and the faces of tankmen blackened by dust and grease. Wherever you looked you saw tanks, self-propelled guns, trucks with infantry, and motorcyclists. We had to move at night. But how long is a night in the beginning of July? Scarcely had the sun gone down in the west when day began to break in the east. Therefore, we were on the move day and night.

And then our moment came.

Along the roads motors roared, clouds of smoke hung in the air, and everywhere hung the smell of diesel oil and burnt rubber.

We were still moving in a column when we heard the thundering of guns. Suddenly we sighted Prokhorovka and a tall grain silo ahead of us.

The deployment of our troops suddenly became complicated because the Germans had driven back the 1st Tank Army and the 6th Guards Army and advanced northward in the zone of defense of the 69th Army.

When we were reconnoitering the terrain south of Prokhorovka, we saw numerous hills, mounds, and ravines which hindered maneuvering by tanks. Having made a round of possible defense lines and positions of the corps, I decided to deploy the units of the army somewhat farther west and southwest of Prokhorovka on a front 10 miles wide, and to have the main blow delivered by four tank corps in the first echelon and by the 5th Mechanized Corps in the second echelon.

The troops were ready for battle.

The units of the 5th Guards Tank Army and the 1st Tank and 6th and 7th Guards armies were to take part in striking a counterblow at Prokhorovka. That had been the plan.

But then the situation changed.

On July 11 the enemy attempted to pin down the 1st Tank Army commanded by General Katukov. But, despite heavy losses, the 1st Tank Army and General Chistyakov's 6th Guards Army continued to repulse the enemy.

The Nazi Command was so confident of success that it was ready to throw in all its reserves for the offensive against Prokhorovka: over 100 Tiger Panzers and Ferdinand self-propelled guns.

About 5:00 P.M., on July 11, Marshal Vasilevsky of the

Supreme Command arrived at the command post of our tank army. I reported to him on the condition of our troops, and together we went to our forward positions.

Although it was toward evening, the bombings by German aircraft did not stop. Riding in a jeep, we crossed a grove and saw the buildings of a state farm on the right. Ahead of us, about one-half mile away, dozens of tanks were moving along the road. Vasilevsky ordered the driver to pull up at the edge of the road and, looking at me sternly, asked me in an unexpectedly sharp voice, for he was usually even-tempered, "General Rotmistrov, what's happening? Why are the tanks moving ahead of time?"

I looked through my binoculars. "They are German tanks."

"Then they may deprive us of our foothold, and, what's more, they may capture Prokhorovka."

I said that we would not let this happen and immediately radioed two tank brigades to advance west of Prokhorovka to disrupt the German action. This was soon accomplished.

The morning of July 12 came. I was at my command post in an orchard southwest of Prokhorovka. The trunks of apple trees were pitted by fragments of bombs and shells. The rods of aerials were protruded from holes dug behind currant bushes.

The quiet of the morning was broken by the roar of Messerschmitts. Columns of smoke soared into the sky from the German bombers. Over 200 advancing Panzers appeared in the northeast.

At 8:00 A.M. a cyclone of fire unleashed by our artillery and rocket launchers swept the entire front of German defenses.

After fifteen minutes of artillery and air bombardment, Soviet tanks left their cover. The 5th Guards Tank Army rushed forward to meet the attacking enemy columns.

Hundreds of vehicles met head-on on a narrow front bound by the Psel River on the one side and a railway embankment on the other.

That was how the famous Battle of Prokhorovka began.

Smoke and dust darkened the sky. Separate shots could not be heard as all sounds blended in a continuous terrific roar: a total of 1,500 tanks were engaged in that battle.

The sun came to our aid. It picked out the contours of the enemy tanks and blinded German tankmen. Our first echelon at full speed cut into the positions of the German troops. The appearance on the battlefield of a great number of our tanks with red stars painted on them threw the Germans into confusion. Control in the advanced German units was soon disrupted. Our tanks were destroying the Tigers at close range, where the Germans could not use their armament to advantage in close combat. We knew their vulnerable spots, so our tank crews were firing at their sides. The shells fired from short distances tore large holes in the armor of the Tigers. Ammunition exploded inside them, and turrets weighing many tons were flung yards away. Thick black smoke rose from the ground.

Displaying heroism and selflessness, the men of the 5th Guards Army under General Zhadov were fighting shoulder to shoulder with the tankmen.

The commander of a tank battalion of the 18th Tank Corps, Captain Skripnik, destroyed two Tigers in a short engagement. But he was wounded and his tank was in flames. The gunner and the driver pulled their wounded commander out of the tank and hid him in a shell crater. The crew of one of the Tigers saw our tankmen and headed toward them. Just in time, the driver jumped back into the burning tank, started the engine, and rushed to meet the Tiger. As the two tanks crashed into each other, they exploded.

In pursuing the enemy, the tank commanded by Soviet officer Mishchenko dashed far ahead and was set on fire. But the crew remained calm, extinguished the flame, and saved the vehicle. The tankmen, who were encircled by the Germans, continued fighting—killing 25 German soldiers—and later returned to their battalion in their own tank.

Over 100 tanks of the SS Totenkopf Division struck at the positions of the 233rd Guards Artillery Regiment. Shpetny, the leader of an antitank rifle platoon, destroyed two German tanks and killed several German submachine gunners. When he ran out of ammunition, the officer, carrying a bunch of grenades, threw himself under a tank, blocking the enemy advance at the cost of his life.

Already as many as 11 tanks were burning in front of a hill. When our artillerymen ran out of shells, they used grenades. All of the heroes died in an unequal fight, but did not surrender the hill. On its approaches, they had destroyed another 16 German tanks.

Directing the battle against the striking tank force of the Germans, I had to watch the southern sector as well.

By 8:00 A.M., the German troops confronting our 69th Army had pressed the units of our two infantry divisions back to the second defense line and began encircling our left flank. Hundreds of enemy tanks might break through to the rear of the army at the height of the battle.

I dispatched our operational reserves to the critical area and later also part of the forces of the second echelon which were so needed at Prokhorovka.

But the enemy was not idle either. By 1:00 P.M. he had brought up the 11th Panzer Division from the reserve, and, together with the SS Totenkopf Division, dealt a powerful blow at our right flank and the defense positions of the 5th Guards Army.

Having no other reserves, I moved two brigades originally intended for developing the offensive to the right flank, to help neighboring units.

Fierce fighting went on unabated until dark. Our 5th Guards Tank Army lost many of its heroes on that day. The tankmen fought to the last. They continued fighting in burning tanks and rammed enemy vehicles.

The enemy sustained tremendous, irreparable losses: the

Germans were losing this battle. Obergruppenführer Hausser, the commander of the SS Panzer Corps, was removed from his post and was blamed for the defeat in the Battle of Kursk.

Over 700 tanks were put out of action on both sides in the battle. Dead bodies, destroyed tanks, crushed guns, and numerous shell craters dotted the battlefield. There was not a single blade of grass to be seen: only burnt, black, and smoldering earth throughout the entire depth of our attack—up to 8 miles.

By 2:00 P.M. on July 12, it was clear that we were winning the battle, albeit slowly. We were pushing the enemy westward, inflicting heavy losses in manpower and materiel, although the Germans had more combat vehicles than we did. Neither the Tigers, Panthers, nor Ferdinands had helped them. The frontal armor of Tigers had a thickness of up to 100 mm and of Ferdinands up to 200 mm. In addition, these vehicles had powerful artillery pieces. The Germans believed that those vehicles were invulnerable. But our T-34 tanks had no equals.

On July 13 Marshal Zhukov visited our army and congratulated the tankmen warmly. We toured the battlefield. Our victory was of tremendous importance since we—but not the enemy—could retrieve and repair damaged vehicles.

On July 16 the armies of the Voronezh Front and on July 19 those of the Steppe Front began pursuing the enemy, and on July 23 they reached the line which our troops had occupied before July 5.

The units of the Bryansk Front and the left wing of the Western Front had driven a wedge into the Germans' defenses on July 12. Tank and infantry units were forcing their way westward to Orel, to devastated villages and towns.

The Germans were retreating. The situation was becoming increasingly grave for the enemy at his Orel springboard. The units of the 3rd Army under General Gorbatov and of the 63rd Army commanded by General Kolpakchi

were engaged in offensive battles on the approaches to
Orel from the east. On August 3 the Military Council of
the Bryansk Front called on officers and men to speed up
the offensive to prevent the Nazis from destroying Orel.

On the same day, August 3, when the troops in the
northern part of the Kursk Bulge were getting ready to
advance on Orel, the units of the Voronezh and Steppe
fronts broke through the enemy defenses after powerful
artillery and air strikes.

Operation Citadel, which had been planned carefully by
the Nazi Command, ended in failure. The giant battle at
Kursk broke the backbone of Nazi Germany and pulver-
ized its crack armored troops.

6. The Liberation of Kiev

Marshal of the Soviet Union Ivan Yakubovsky (1912–1976) served in the Soviet Army from 1932. In the Second World War, he was the commander of a tank battalion, a regiment, a brigade, and a deputy corps commander. After the war, he commanded a tank division, the armored forces of a military district, and was the Supreme Commander of the Soviet Forces in Germany and later of the Joint Armed Forces of the Warsaw Treaty countries. The battle described below occurred at a time when he was a tank brigade commander.

Late into the night of October 24, 1943, the GHQ mapped out in detail the mission assigned earlier to the forces of the First Ukrainian Front for the routing of the enemy grouping in the area of Kiev and the liberation of the Ukraine's capital.

Having made a thorough analysis of the shortcomings of the previous offensive, the GHQ ordered a new direction for troop concentration in the Kiev offensive operation. The main attack was to be launched on November 1 and 2 by the right flank north of Kiev, instead of from the Veliky Bukrin bridgehead, where the enemy had amassed a strong grouping during the October fighting and where the terrain was difficult for the large-scale use of tanks. The troops ordered to pin down as much of the enemy force as possible south of Kiev were also ordered to resume their offensive and to break through the enemy's defenses when conditions became favorable.

It was a difficult mission. Over 300 tanks and self-propelled guns, hundreds of artillery pieces, armored personnel carriers, and motor vehicles had to be moved quickly and secretly from the Veliky Bukrin bridgehead, then for nearly 125 miles along the front line and, finally, across the Desna and again across the Dnieper to another bridgehead.

My 91st Separate Tank Brigade was to be among the first to advance and cross the Dnieper to get to its eastern bank. We had our hands full. Our success depended on clockwork precision at all command levels and a sense of purpose in the actions of every officer and man. I was pleased to note that the staff, the officers and men in the battalions, and the supporting services were doing their job with great energy, not held back by difficulties.

Our 3rd Guards Tank Army began regrouping. The crucial task was to move the troops from the Veliky Bukrin bridgehead to the left bank of the Dnieper.

A thick fog over the river provided good cover, but it also slowed down our crossing. At times ferries went along the river for 30 to 40 minutes, only to find themselves at their original piers. The fog lifted only on the morning of October 27. When gray weather with low clouds set in, it became possible to move over the remaining tanks. Early the next morning, the entire 3rd Guards Tank Army was assembled on the eastern bank of the Dnieper. Its units, having reached the starting points of their routes or areas close to them, immediately began to prepare for a night march.

The path along the Dnieper defense lines, which brought back memories of the terrible autumn of 1941, was by no means easy. Among the officers and men who had battled their way from the Volga and the Caucasus to Kiev were many who remembered those grim days: fierce fighting at the Dnieper and the forced retreat from Kiev.

That was one of the dramatic events of the first months of the war. A critical situation had developed in the Kiev sector in mid-September, and the city was abandoned on September 19. The main forces of the Southwestern Front together with its staff were encircled. Front Commander Colonel-General Kirponos ordered his troops to break out of the ring, but the effort failed.

The officers and men of the staffs of the Southwestern Front and the 5th Army, breaking out of the enemy encirclement, engaged in battle against heavy odds in the Shumeikovo grove on September 20. The group numbered about 2,000, including 800 commanders and staff officers. Among them were Front Commander Colonel-General Kirponos, members of the Front Military Council Burmistenko and Rykov, Chief of the Front Staff Major-General Tupikov, Commander of the Front Air Force Colonel-General Astakhov, Commander of the 5th Army Major-General Potapov, and other generals.

Having entered a deep ravine in the grove, the staff column found itself trapped. The enemy, sensing a big catch, followed immediately. An enemy reconnaissance plane appeared over the grove at noon on September 20. It was clear that battle could not be avoided. The commanders, staff officers, and soldiers armed with pistols, rifles, and hand grenades took up perimeter defense positions at the edge of the grove. They had several armored cars, antitank guns, and quadruple-mount antiaircraft machine guns.

Half an hour later, the enemy made his first mortar assault on the grove, followed by an attack of tanks and submachine gunners. A bloody battle broke out. At first the Nazis managed to penetrate our defense positions, but were beaten back. A second attack was also repulsed, but at heavy cost in lives. General Kirponos had his leg broken by a shell fragment. He was carried to the bottom of the ravine and laid near a spring. Meanwhile the battle raged on. The Front Military Council held its last meeting around 7:00 P.M. to discuss ways of breaking out of the ring. Just at that moment, the enemy launched yet another mortar assault and one of the mines exploded near the spring where the group had assembled. Many were killed. General Kirponos received mortal wounds in the chest and head and died a few minutes later.

. . . Two years had passed since those gigantic, unprecedentedly bloody battles were fought. Then came the autumn of 1943. Again our forces were at the Dnieper.

We moved from Veliky Bukrin to Lyutezh at night, in rain and mud. To have completed the march was almost like winning a battle. Despite the tremendous strain, each of us realized that the success of our maneuver would ensure victory on the right bank.

As before, the forces of the First Ukrainian Front were opposed by the 2nd Army of German Army Group Center, the 4th Panzer Army, and units of the 8th Army of Army Group South. The enemy had a large air force grouping in the attack zone which was part of the 4th Air Fleet. All told, the forces of the First Ukrainian Front faced 33 German division, about 6,000 guns and mortars, nearly 400 tanks and self-propelled guns, and 665 aircraft.

In a bid to halt the Soviet advance at all costs, the Nazi Command launched frantic activities to build up its defense lines. When the Soviet troops crossed the river, the enemy went over to rigid defense in a desperate attempt to hold his positions and prevent us from widening our bridgeheads on the right bank of the Dnieper.

By the start of the offensive, the First Ukrainian Front numbered over 660,000 troops, about 7,000 guns and mortars, 675 tanks and self-propelled guns, and 700 combat planes. Although overall Soviet superiority was not considerable, a daring maneuver to regroup forces in the main direction of the attack made it possible to outweigh the enemy decisively.

The commander of the First Ukrainian Front ordered the 38th Army of Colonel-General Moskalenko to move on Kiev from the north. Its mission was to envelop the city from the west and to capture it. Its neighbor on the right flank, the 60th Army under the command of Lieutenant-General Chernyakhovsky, was to deliver a strike between the Zdvizh and Irpen rivers.

The mobile troops were assigned an important role in the offensive operation. The 3rd Guards Tank Army and the 1st Guards Cavalry Corps under its operational command from October 28 were to enter the breach in the enemy defense lines in the 38th Army zone and push on the attack toward the southwest.

When the Front Commander, General of the Army Vatutin, explained the combat missions to the army, corps, and brigade commanders, he emphasized the need for a swift and surprise armored attack from the Lyutezh bridgehead. I was present at the briefing and was deeply moved by words of the eminent general, who spoke with confidence in our victory:

"Speed and resolution in breaking through the enemy defense—this is what will ensure our success," said the commander quietly. "For if we fail to do so, the enemy will have time to move over his troops from Bukrin, and we'll have much tougher going then."

Most of the tank units were amassed in the main direction of the thrust north of Kiev, where the 5th Guards Tank Corps and the 3rd Guards Tank Army operated. Our tank army was used as a front mobile group, while the tank corps acted as the mobile groups of the armies. Separate tank brigades and regiments were attached to large rifle units in the main direction of the attack to be used as direct infantry support tanks.

Much was done to ensure secrecy of our preparations. Besides camouflaging the left flank of the front to cover up the regrouping of forces, the concentration of a huge number of troops was simulated on the right flank, in the 13th Army zone. Among other things, 200 mockup tanks were set up in the area between the Dnieper and Pripyat rivers to make it appear that the forces of the front were going to deliver the main blow in that sector. All in all, in early November 1943, the engineer troops set up 687 mockup tanks, 143 mockup guns, and 115 mockup motor vehicles.

To mislead the enemy further about the size of our forces in the mock concentration area, several radio stations were ordered to get busy to create the impression that the headquarters of a tank corps was situated there. At the same time, the units of the 129th Tank Brigade were continually on the move. Other cover-up measures included reconnaissance of the banks of the River Pripyat, spreading false rumors about an imminent attack in the 13th Army zone, and engineer work along the River Pripyat—bringing in timber, the construction of bypass roads, and other work.

The steps taken to confuse the enemy about the impending operation—its objective, scale, and timing—proved effective. The enemy failed to determine the main direction of our thrust and its timing in advance.

The offensive started on November 1, 1943, by a strike from the Veliky Bukrin bridgehead. Fierce fighting broke out at once. The enemy fought back ferociously, launching frequent counterattacks.

In the first day of the battle, the advancing 40th and 27th armies failed to cope with their missions. Bad weather prevented the air force units from giving effective assistance to our land troops. Nor were those armies successful the following day. Nevertheless, the front commander, seeking to mislead the enemy about the main direction of the attack, ordered them to continue operations in the Veliky Bukrin sector.

The stratagem worked. The enemy did not pull a single division out of that area. Moreover, the German Command moved its reserves to Veliky Bukrin: the Reich SS Panzer Division, the 223rd Infantry Division, and one regiment from the 168th Infantry Division.

Action in the main sector north of Kiev got under way on November 3. Separate tank regiments and brigades as well as part of the forces of the 5th Guards Tank Corps, which were giving direct support to the infantry of the 38th Army, moved to their starting lines on the night before the attack. Engineering units cleared passages in the minefields. Aircraft of the night bomber division pounded the enemy positions from dusk to dawn.

Our troops went into attack at 8:40 A.M. following a heavy artillery preparation. The defense lines were broken through in the 38th Army attack zone in the sectors of the 50th and 51st Rifle Corps.

The 24th and 30th Rifle Corps of the 60th Army also did well, developing a swift thrust deep into the enemy lines. The tank units greatly helped the infantry.

On the first day of the attack, the armies under Generals Moskalenko and Chernyakhovsky broke through the main enemy defense line and engaged in a battle to breach the second defense line.

In the first twelve hours of November 4, the 3rd Guards Tank Army began to move to its starting positions to be brought into the breach. Together with the 38th Army, it was to rout the opposing enemy grouping in the tactical zone of its defenses, cut off the Zhitomir highway, and later develop the attack on Fastov and Vasilkovo, to envelop the enemy force from the west in the Kiev area.

The 9th Mechanized Corps was ordered to enter the breach following the 23rd Rifle Corps, overtake the infantry units, and capture an area on the eastern bank of the River Irpen toward the evening of November 4. The 6th Guards Tank Corps was temporarily to turn over two of its brigades to the 50th Rifle Corps for direct infantry support until the infantry units were overtaken. After that it was to attack the enemy in full force.

After a brief fire assault by artillery and bombing strikes at noon on November 4, the tank army units began their offensive. At first, only the 52nd and 53rd Guards Tank Brigades positioned inside the battle formations of the rifle divisions went into action.

By evening, the tank army units had advanced up to 5 miles in the southwest. General Rybalko decided to continue the advance at night. However, a thick fog descended in the evening so that one could not see houses, trees, or roads even within a couple of yards. It would not be safe to move in pitch-darkness.

My brigade decided to let the tanks move ahead with the headlights switched on. Before doing that, however, we checked to make sure that the lights would not reveal our battle formations to the enemy.

Then the attack began. Beams of light suddenly rained down on the enemy from the dark, exposing his fortifications. With their sirens howling, tanks from our brigade carrying submachine gunners rushed on the enemy firing their cannon and machine guns on the go.

It was a staggering picture. At first the Nazis were stunned and thrown into total confusion. A brief panic— that was all the tankmen needed to complete their job with success.

After breaking through the tactical zone of the enemy defense, the tank and mechanized units of the 3rd Guards Tank Army rolled down to the south.

By the next morning, our forces had cut off the Kiev-Zhitomir railway line and motorway which was the main transport artery of the enemy grouping at Kiev. The tank army's reaching the area west of Kiev was of crucial importance for the liberation of the city and the routing of the enemy there. Our troops had prevented the enemy from bringing up reserves and equipment, and, what was crucial, had blocked the way for the Nazi retreat to the west. The enemy defense system around Kiev was disrupted, and it became possible to strike at the Nazis from the rear.

Fierce fighting broke out at the northern approaches to Kiev on November 5 in the attack zone of the 38th Army.

The battle for Kiev grew in ferocity by the hour. The enemy held on to every hill and village, fighting back desperately. Large Nazi Panzer and infantry forces counterattacked our advancing troops several times. However, the vigorous action of the 5th Guards Tank Corps broke the enemy resistance. Its units reached Kiev's northern and western outskirts in the afternoon.

Thus, in the course of a bitter battle on November 5, the 38th Army, together with the 3rd Guards Tank Army, fought its way forward up to 15 miles and created the necessary conditions for a decisive assault on Kiev and for developing the offensive of the front's forces to widen the Kiev strategic bridgehead.

The 51st Rifle Corps battled in the northern outskirts of the city. The 1st Czechoslovak Separate Brigade, under Colonel Ludvik Svoboda, fought together with the corps units. The Front Military Council showed particular care and attention toward the brigade, and it was committed to battle only after several persistent requests from Colonel Svoboda. He told his men: "Fight for Kiev the way you would fight for Prague and Bratislava." And the Czechoslovak soldiers acquitted themselves with honor in carrying out his order.

The 60th Army also scored considerable success on November 5. Its left flank advanced up to 13 miles and captured 17 populated areas. However, it failed to exploit the success and expand the bridgehead. The enemy put up stiff resistance.

The situation in this area where the right-flank units of General Moskalenko's 38th Army were also engaged in battle had become more complicated. The enemy was preparing to strike a counterblow on those units.

However, the corps units, having broken through the enemy defenses, rolled westward from the morning of November 7. Shortly afterward, the left-flank units of the

60th Army and of the 1st Guards Cavalry Corps fully averted the threat of an enemy counterblow from the northwest at the strike grouping of the 38th Army operating in the Kiev area.

The hour of the final battle for Kiev was approaching. To speed up the liberation of the city, the front commander decided to reinforce the strike grouping with units from the 13th, 27th, and 40th armies.

Kiev was ablaze with the red glow of fires. Houses, shops, factories—everything was burning. Soviet troops, in order to minimize damage to the city and its population, rushed toward the city center. Breaking enemy resistance, they captured block by block, street by street from the Nazis. The night was turned into day by thousands of flares, flashes of artillery and mortar salvos, and fires.

That was how the crucial battle for Kiev got under way. Shortly afterward, the armored vehicles of the 5th Guards Tank Corps, the 39th Separate Tank Regiment, and the tank battalion of the 1st Czechoslovak Brigade with submachine gunners on board reached the city center. They took over the Government House, the central post office, the bank, the railway terminal, and the main communications centers. The capital of the Ukraine was liberated from the enemy by 4:00 A.M. on November 6.

The initial German attack: June 22, 1941

Preparation for the defense of Moscow: Red Army theater in the background

Red Army headquarters in Stalingrad—only a few hundred yards from Von Paulus's headquarters (General Vasili Chuikov, second from left)

Prisoners: the remnants of Von Paulus's Sixth Army

Soviet tanks lifting the siege of Leningrad

General Rotmistrov at the front in 1943

Russian staff planning strategy near the front

A commander leads an attack

A ship in the Crimea breaks away under cover of a smoke screen

Torpedoes were used to destroy the walls of Königsberg castle

In Budapest, a symbol of victory

General Keitel's official surrender

Marshall Zhukov and British Air Marshall Teddar signing the surrender document

German prisoners being marched along the silent streets of Moscow

Soviet and American officers compare their routes to Berlin

The Japanese surrender

The victorious Allied commanders

The premature end of The Thousand-Year Reich (Berlin)

7. The Korsun-Shevchenkovsky Pocket

Marshal of the Soviet Union Ivan Konev (1897–1973) was called up for army service as a private in 1916. He was an army commander when the Second World War broke out. From the autumn of 1941 to the end of the war, he successively commanded the forces of several fronts. After the war, Marshal Konev was Commander-in-Chief of the Soviet Union's Land Forces, then commanded the troops of a military district. Later he was appointed Commander-in-Chief of the Joint Armed Forces of the Warsaw Treaty countries and Inspector General of the USSR Defense Ministry.

In early 1944 the forces of the Second Ukrainian Front under my command captured a large bridgehead west and northwest of Dnepropetrovsk and, following the Kirovograd offensive operation, pushed the enemy back from the Dnieper more than 65 miles.

However, the Nazis managed to hold on to their positions in the middle reaches of the Dnieper near Kanev. As a result, there emerged what became known as the Korsun-Shevchenkovsky pocket. Using favorable terrain, the defending German troops hung over the adjoining flanks of our fronts and denied them freedom to maneuver.

Hitler's GHQ and the Command of Army Group South hoped that with the start of the muddy season, the Soviet troops would not be able to advance on a large scale as previously and that the bad weather would give the Germans a respite in the southern sector of their Eastern Front. The enemy still thought that he might be able to push our forces back to the Dnieper by a series of heavy blows, hold on to the rich industrial and farming areas of the Ukraine on the right bank of the Dnieper, and establish land links with his Crimean grouping. Hitler did everything to hang on to the regions on the right bank of the Dnieper, realizing full well that their loss would break the whole of the German strategic front. The desire to hold positions at the Dnieper was in no small measure dictated by propaganda considerations, by an attempt to conceal the collapse of his strategic plans on the Eastern Front.

In view of the strategic importance attached to the right-bank Ukraine, the Nazi Command had amassed large numbers of its more combat-efficient units and formations in the area: 93 divisions in all, including 18 Panzer divisions out of the total of 25 operating on the entire Soviet-German front.

The Korsun-Shevchenkovsky pocket was defended by the right-flank units of the 1st Panzer Army and the left-flank units of the 8th Field Army, consisting of 9 infantry and 1 tank divisions, a motorized brigade, and 4 assault gun battalions.

To prevent the enemy from fortifying his defenses and strengthening his grouping, we had to start eliminating the Korsun-Shevchenkovsky pocket as soon as possible. Preparations had to be made quickly. The fronts, including the Second Ukrainian Front, had to regroup large forces in difficult conditions. We had to transfer the main forces, including the 5th Guards Tank Army operating on the left flank of the front near Kirovograd, where the fighting had just ended, to the north quickly and secretly and prepare for attack.

Both the weather and the terrain were exceptionally unfavorable for preparing the operation. The sudden thaw and the muddy roads made it more difficult to move troops and to supply them with fuel and ammunition.

In planning the operations of the Second Ukrainian Front, we took into account the fact that the area west and northwest of Kirovograd had the heaviest concentration of enemy troops following the operation that had recently ended there. Evidently, the German Command was expecting our further offensive there and had kept a strong Panzer force in the area.

Bearing all that in mind, I decided that the main blow should be delivered north of Kirovograd by the adjoining flanks of the 4th Guards Army and the 53rd Army, totaling 14 rifle divisions supported by the front's air-force units. After breaking through the enemy defenses in the 12-mile sector of Verbovka and Vasilyevka, those armies were to push their attack to Shpola and Zvenigorodka. The 4th Guards Army was to attack the inner front while the 53rd Army attacked the outer front.

The 5th Guards Tank Army, which had 218 tanks and 18 self-propelled guns, was to be committed to battle in the zone of the 53rd Army. Its mission was to complete the breakthrough of the enemy defenses and, pushing ahead rapidly, reach the Shpola area toward the evening of the second day. Later it was to link up with the mobile forces of the First Ukrainian Front and capture Zvenigorodka, complete the encirclement, and form the outer front together with the 53rd Army.

In addition to the main attack, two auxiliary blows were to be delivered by the 5th and 7th Guards Armies west and southwest of Kirovograd and by the 52nd Army in the direction of Maloye Staroselye and Gorodishche.

The strike force of the First Ukrainian Front, consisting of some of the units of the 40th Army and the 6th Tank Army, was to advance from an area southeast of Belaya Tserkov toward Zvenigorodka. The 6th Tank Army's mission was to develop the offensive and link up with the tank force of the Second Ukrainian Front near Zvenigorodka.

Air cover and support were to be provided by the 2nd and 5th Air armies. The strikes by bombers and attack planes would help the troops break through the enemy defenses, make sure that the tank armies entered the breach, destroy enemy aircraft in the battlefield, and provide cover for the battle formations of our troops.

To ensure surprise, strict measures for camouflage and for misleading the enemy were taken in the regrouping of our forces in the main direction of the attack. We set up dummy tank and artillery concentration areas, dummy fire positions, and simulated troop and tank movements. All of these greatly contributed to the success of the operation.

The offensive began on January 24. To avoid the artillery preparation directed against the enemy's covering forces and detect the true location of his main defense zone, we decided to launch a brief but powerful artillery attack, followed immediately by the offensive of the advance battalions. If they succeeded, the main forces of the front's strike grouping were to be committed. The advance battalions mounted a surprise attack at dawn. They broke through the enemy defenses in a 6-mile sector and advanced 1 to 4 miles.

Next we committed the main forces of the 4th Guards Army and the 53rd Army. The breakthrough was developed successfully. After heavy fighting for strongpoints and centers of resistance, the Soviet troops penetrated the enemy defenses to a depth of 2½ to 6 miles on the first day of the operation: they had forced their way through the first defense zone. The 5th Guards Tank Army committed to action in the afternoon exploited the success by forging ahead 10 to 12 miles by evening. Having become separated from the rifle units, it crossed the enemy's second defense line, consolidated its hold on the captured positions, and turned its left-flank units southward to widen the breach toward the flanks.

When the Nazis had detected the main direction of our attack and realized the serious threat to the whole of their grouping, they began hastily to gather their forces to frustrate our offensive. Panzer divisions were transferred from the Kirovograd sector to the combat area. Strong strike groups were formed hastily on the flanks of our breach.

However, those measures did not take us by surprise. We knew from experience that the Nazi Command would by all means try to cut off our advancing troops at the base of the breach. Therefore the 4th and 53rd armies had a sufficiently deep operational formation while the tank army advanced in two waves. In addition, the front had also formed operational reserves.

As we had expected, both enemy groupings mounted an offensive on January 27 from the north and south. Evidently, by delivering a simultaneous strike at our flanks, the enemy hoped to seal off the breach in the defenses and cut off our tank units, which had reached the Shpola area by that time, from the main forces of the front.

Fierce battles began throughout the area of the breach. The Soviet troops beat off successive enemy counterattacks with courage and staunchness. Our artillery and tank units played an exceptionally important part in the battle. There were so many truly heroic exploits in those intense hours of fighting.

Commander of the 5th Guards Tank Army Colonel-General Rotmistrov displayed notable self-control and combat maturity. When I arrived at his command post on a height at Ositnyazhka I saw that the situation was far from pleasant. The cannonade kept booming, submachine and machine-gun bursts were heard quite closely, and shells exploded and bullets whistled all over the place. In those critical conditions, General Rotmistrov directed the actions of his units with great precision, assessing the situation realistically and making sound decisions.

The commitment of the second wave—the 18th Tank Corps—helped us quickly to clear the breach, protect our flanks, and continue the offensive toward Zvenigorodka. In addition, fresh forces from the front's reserves were brought in to seal off the breach in the flanks.

The 5th Guards Don Cavalry Corps was to be committed to action on the night of January 28. Its mission was to strike at the enemy rear, and, advancing in the general direction of Olshana, to destroy his manpower and materiel, disrupt troop control, and, in coordination with tank units and the left-flank units of the 27th Army of the First Ukrainian Front, to prevent the enemy's Korsun-Shevchenkovsky grouping from retreating south.

The entire experience of the past war shows that to encircle an active, maneuverable, and well-equipped enemy force is by no means an easy job for commanders and their superiors at all levels. It requires high military skills. The situation during the Korsun-Shevchenkovsky encirclement operation was highly volatile, and it was necessary to determine the main points quickly and make prompt decisions. There were many dangers and surprises. It was necessary to reinforce troops that were widening the breach and cutting through the enemy defense lines, take steps to repulse flanking attacks at the base of the breach, and commit troops to set up the outer and inner rings of encirclement. The need for additional forces and reserves increases continuously in the course of any battle. That is exactly what the second echelons and reserves are set up for. And this need becomes immeasurably greater in encirclement operations.

Therefore it became necessary extensively to maneuver troops and to remove units from the unattacked sectors.

The timely measures taken enabled the Second Ukrainian Front not only to repulse fierce attacks and counterattacks by large enemy forces on the flanks of the breach, but also to pursue the offensive with success and complete the encirclement of the enemy, beating off his massive attacks on the outer front while cutting the encircled troops into small parts.

On January 28, the 20th Guards Corps of the 5th Guards Tank Army, which was advancing swiftly with its two brigades, reached Zvenigorodka. To meet them, the 233rd Tank Brigade and other advance units of the 6th Tank Army of the First Ukrainian Front broke through the enemy lines from the west.

Thus the ring of our forces closed at Zvenigorodka, marking the beginning of the encirclement of the entire German Korsun-Shevchenkovsky pocket.

The outer ring of encirclement was being formed under difficult conditions. The Nazi troops were delivering counterblows all the time and, as a result, the continuous outer ring was formed later, after the Soviet mobile forces linked up near Zvenigorodka.

The mission of the First and Second Ukrainian fronts was to destroy the encircled grouping while repulsing counterblows on the outer ring.

What was the composition of the Soviet and enemy forces?

The Soviet forces had a total of 22 rifle divisions, 2,736 guns and mortars, and two tank armies with 307 tanks and self-propelled guns on the outer ring, about 95 miles long, stretching from Okhmatov to Kanizh. The operational density was one division for every 4.25 miles, and 29 artillery pieces, 3 tanks, and self-propelled guns for every mile of the front.

The enemy force on the outer ring consisted of 14 divisions, including 8 Panzer divisions, with a density of one division for every 5.5 miles. It should be pointed out that the German divisions outnumbered the Soviet ones in strength almost twofold.

The correlation of forces on the outer ring in the number of divisions was 1.3:1 in our favor, whereas the enemy outnumbered the Soviet forces in tanks. Under those circumstances, the Soviet troops on the outer ring could not advance southwest and simultaneously destroy the encircled enemy grouping. Therefore they assumed stable defense until the rout of the encircled enemy forces was completed.

A solid inner ring of encirclement was formed by January 31. The trapped enemy force consisted of units of 10 divisions and one brigade numbering about 80,000 officers and men, with up to 1,600 guns and mortars, more than 230 tanks and assault guns, and many other weapons.

The enemy began to bring up Panzer units to rescue his surrounded divisions. For instance, the Nazis concentrated four Panzer divisions of their 8th Army in the area of Novo-Mirgorod.

Fierce fighting raged from February 1 to 3. Having concentrated four Panzer divisions (the 13th, 11th, 3rd, and 14th) in the Yurkovka-Lisyanka sector, the Nazis launched the offensive on the morning of February 4 against the 5th Guards Tank Army and the 53rd Army. On the same day, the encircled enemy struck in the direction of Burta with a force of up to two infantry divisions and one regiment of the 14th Panzer Division to meet the Panzer grouping advancing toward Krymka from the outer ring. As a result, the Nazis were able to push our forces 3 miles north.

During the first week of February, the enemy persisted in launching Panzer attacks from the outer ring. However, the Soviet forces invariably countered the enemy armored thrust with an insurmountable barrier of artillery and tank fire.

All Nazi attempts to break through the outer ring of encirclement in the zone of our front failed. Having run into impenetrable artillery and tank defense in this sector, the Nazis began to shift their attacks from the east to the west to the zone of the First Ukrainian Front.

It was clear that the Nazi Command would keep up its pressure from both the outer and the inner ring. Particularly vigorous action was expected in the zone of the First Ukrainian Front.

Having brought up eight Panzer and six infantry divisions to the outer ring and changing the direction of its strikes, the enemy tried to burst through the Soviet defenses in a narrow (9-mile) sector by four Panzer divisions (the SS Adolf Hitler Division, and the 17th, 1st, and 16th) and two infantry divisions.

At the cost of heavy losses, the Nazis managed to drive a wedge into Soviet defense lines in the zone of the 47th Rifle Corps of the First Ukrainian Front near Rizino. At the same time, the Nazis continued their Panzer attacks in the zone of our front in the area of Yerki in the general direction of Lisyanka. However, they were beaten off by the 5th Guards Tank Army and the 49th Rifle Corps.

The situation was becoming critical. The enemy tried his utmost to break through our outer ring and link up with his surrounded troops. But the very idea that the Nazis could get through at the juncture of the fronts or through the neighboring front was inadmissible.

I then decided that it would be necessary to move General Rotmistrov's army from the outer ring to the corridor near Lisyanka where the enemy was making desperate attempts to rescue his trapped units.

The Command of the First Ukrainian Front also took appropriate measures by moving rifle units and artillery to the area of Vinograd and Lisyanka. The 2nd Tank Army of the GHQ reserve was also moved to that sector.

Through powerful strikes of their Panzer divisions, the Nazi generals hoped to break out of the encirclement and regain their previous positions. Manstein, who had tried unsuccessfully to rescue von Paulus's army surrounded at Stalingrad, was eager to give a good account of himself this time and make a brilliant display of his military talent. Obviously remembering that in the Stalingrad operation his Army Group Hoth sent to rescue Paulus took a sound beating from the Soviet Army, Manstein decided to form a strong grouping consisting, as mentioned earlier, of eight Panzer and six infantry divisions. Army Group Hoth at

Stalingrad had only four Panzer divisions, one motorized, and nine infantry divisions.

While completing the encirclement and beating off Panzer attacks on the outer ring, the First and Second Ukrainian Fronts mounted a vigorous offensive on the inner ring to cut and destroy the trapped enemy units.

The fighting was especially fierce. The enemy held tenaciously on to every defense line, to every populated area. Overcoming frantic enemy resistance, the Soviet troops forged ahead, tightening the iron grip on the encircled Germans. It should be noted that at this point the Nazis inside the trap had not yet lost their fighting efficiency.

The Nazi Command tried to supply the encircled forces with food, fuel, and ammunition by air. But the Soviet air force and antiaircraft artillery almost completely frustrated these attempts. About 200 enemy cargo planes were destroyed over several days.

To avoid unnecessary bloodshed, on February 8 the Soviet command presented the surrounded forces with an ultimatum to lay down arms.

However, the Nazi generals rejected this humanitarian proposal, and fighting resumed with renewed force. Far from stopping their resistance, the German forces began to launch attacks in a number of sectors with even greater ferocity. Ignoring enormous casualties, the German generals and officers sought to get out of the trap in order to save their regimental honor, if not their own lives and the lives of their men.

How was the operation completed? On February 10 I took the final decision to move the 5th Guards Tank Army from the outer ring to the corridor and ordered it to prevent the enemy grouping from breaking out of the pocket at the juncture of the two fronts and linking up with the Panzer force advancing from the outer ring.

Intense fighting with intermittent success went on all along the sector of the 2nd and 6th Tank armies throughout February 10 and 11. On the morning of February 11, the enemy attacked the 6th Tank Army units with 200 tanks and infantry. Overcoming the stiff resistance of the First Ukrainian Front, the enemy reached the Frankovka-Buzhanka sector in the evening. Bitter fighting in that sector continued on February 12.

Meanwhile General Stemmermann had hastily been forming a strike force consisting of a combat group of the reserve 332nd Infantry Division stationed in the Korsun-Shevchenkovsky area and the 72nd Infantry Division reinforced by a Panzer battalion of the SS Viking Division, a motorized regiment, and the Walonia SS Motorized Brigade. These forces launched the offensive in the morning of February 12 in the sector of the 27th Army of the First Ukrainian Front, striking the blow at Shenderovka from the area of Steblev in the hope of breaking through the front to link up with the German troops mounting an attack on Lisyanka.

Disregarding losses, the enemy rushed into battle with the desperation of the doomed. The Nazis succeeded in breaking through the defenses of the 27th Army, which unfortunately was under strength and held a broad front. The distance between the encircled grouping and the enemy troops advancing on the outer ring was reduced to 7 miles. The danger arose that they might break out of the encirclement. It was the most critical phase of the operation.

The GHQ expressed concern over the breakthrough of the enemy forces. The Supreme Commander called me up over the high-frequency network about midday on February 12, 1944.

Stalin was angry. He said we had loudly announced for all the world to hear that a large enemy grouping was surrounded in the area of Korsun-Shevchenkovsky, and yet the GHQ had information that the encircled Germans had broken through the front of the 27th Army and was moving toward their own forces. "What do you know about the situation on the neighboring front?" he demanded.

I realized from his sharp tone that the Supreme Commander was alarmed and that someone had evidently given him a slightly inaccurate report.

I replied, "There is no need to worry, Comrade Stalin. The encircled enemy will not escape. Our front has taken the necessary steps. I have moved units of the 5th Guards Tank Army and the 5th Cavalry Corps to the sector of the Germans' breakthrough to drive them back into the trap and to secure a linkup with the First Ukrainian Front."

All the armies of the front were ready to take swift, vigorous action to cut and destroy or capture the enemy forces. Furthermore, I issued orders that antitank defenses be fortified all through the corridor by setting up tankproof areas with land mines and other obstacles. Tankproof areas were set up at all vital road junctions, populated centers, and heights. They were in the charge of artillery regiment or antitank artillery brigade commanders. It may be pointed out here that the antitank brigades gave an exceptionally good account of themselves in the Great Patriotic War. When we sent the brigades to the tank-threatened locations, we were always confident that their trained personnel and combat experience would put up staunch resistance and inflict heavy losses on the enemy.

The First Ukrainian Front also stepped up its operations simultaneously with the forces of the Second Ukrainian Front. The Command also took vigorous measures to prevent the enemy tank grouping from linking up with the surrounded troops.

The Second Ukrainian Front, which had been engaged in intense fighting, tightened the noose to the limit toward the evening of February 16.

Reconnaissance data indicated that the Nazis would try to break out of the trap. Since they were driven into a small area, they could make only one of two moves: surrender or force their way through. Having lost all hope for outside help, the command of the encircled troops decided to launch a last desperate attempt to escape from the trap.

The battle formation of the attacking forces was made up of several echelons. Assigned to the first echelon were the 72nd and 112th Infantry Divisions and the SS Viking Panzer Division. Immediately behind the units of the SS Viking Division came the command of the encircled grouping, staffs of large units and officers up to regimental commanders under the cover of assault guns and submachine gunners. Following them were trains with the wounded and medical units.

The rest of the encircled units, big and small, made up the second echelon. The 83rd Infantry Division was to provide cover from the north and east. The 57th Infantry Division had the same mission in the south.

The broad Nazi columns moved toward our positions at 3:00 A.M. on February 17. The enemy onslaught was taken by the 27th Army and the 4th Guards Army. The 18th and 29th Tank Corps and the 5th Guards Cavalry Corps were immediately ordered to advance toward each other and capture or destroy enemy troops.

It was impossible for the Nazis to burst through four defense lines: two on the inner ring of the encirclement and two on the outer one, and to bypass tankproof areas and artillery in the center of the corridor. Again the tankproof areas played their great role.

However, it was not only the heavy artillery barrages that blocked the German attempt to break out of the trap. The Nazis trying to escape from the pocket came under the blows not only of the defending troops, but chiefly of reserves, mobile strike groups, tank corps, and a cavalry corps.

The tanks operated with turned-on headlights, closing in on the enemy troops both by fire and maneuver and blocking their frantic attempts to get out of the ring. From dawn onward, the Cossacks were in the battlefield with drawn swords, chasing the Nazis and taking them prisoner. Infantrymen were engaged in hand-to-hand fighting using bayonets, submachine guns, and carbines.

At sunrise, the Nazis, realizing that their situation was utterly hopeless, began to surrender in large groups. While the battle was raging, I spoke several times over the phone with the commanders of the 69th, 7th, and 41st Divisions holding positions along the bank of the River Gorny Tikich on the outer ring of the trap. They reported that not a single German soldier had crossed their lines.

By morning, the enemy position was wiped out. Tens of thousands of German soldiers had paid with their lives for the senseless and criminal stubbornness of their Nazi commanders who had rejected our ultimatum to surrender on February 8.

It was reported to me that General Stemmermann was killed during the German attempt to break out of the trap on the night of February 17, 1944. His body was found on the battlefield.

According to official figures, the enemy lost 55,000 officers and men killed, more than 18,000 taken prisoner, and large quantities of weapons and other military equipment. It must be pointed out that these figures do not fully reflect the enemy's total casualties. For example, in their attempt to break through the encirclement from the outside, the Germans lost 20,000 officers and men killed and large quantities of materiel, including 329 aircraft and more than 600 tanks and 500 guns.

The success of the operation made it possible to push the enemy away from the Dnieper for good. All hopes of the Nazis to rebuild their defenses in the middle reaches of the river were dashed. The Soviet forces found themselves in a favorable situation for further operations in the right-bank Ukraine and for freeing the entire south from the Nazi invaders.

After my brief report to the GHQ by phone on the completion of the battle at Korsun-Shevchenkovsky, Stalin said, "Congratulations. The government wishes to give you the rank of Marshal of the Soviet Union. What do you think of it? Any objections? May I congratulate you?"

All I could say was "Thank you, Comrade Stalin." I heard over the radio of a decree to confer the rank of marshal on me while I was at General Rotmistrov's command post. Congratulations showered on me from all sides. Rotmistrov happened to have a bottle of port, and we celebrated that important landmark in my life modestly, but with great joy.

The following day, the marshal's shoulder pieces were brought to me by plane. They came from Marshal Georgi Zhukov. It was a sign of attention, a message of congratulations, and a priceless gift.

8. Operation Bagration

Marshal of the Soviet Union Konstantin Rokossovsky (1896–
1968) served in the armed forces since 1914. At the start of
the Second World War, he commanded a mechanized corps
and then an army. From the summer of 1942 until the end
of the war, he was the commander of a number of fronts.
After the war he commanded the troops of a military district,
was a Deputy Minister of Defense, and was the Inspector
General of the Ministry of Defense. From 1949 to 1956 he
was Poland's Minister of National Defense (he was a Pole by
nationality).

During Operation Bagration he commanded the troops of
the First Byelorussian Front.

By the spring of 1944, our troops in the Ukraine had
pushed a long way forward. Then the enemy brought
up fresh forces from the west and halted our advance. The
fighting became protracted, and this compelled the general
staff and GHQ to shift the main effort to a new sector.

We decided that the main effort was bound to shift to
the western strategic areas and that the forthcoming campaign would develop in Byelorussia. Our troops would be
able to reach very important lines by the shortest routes

and thus create favorable conditions for striking at the enemy in other sectors.

In March Supreme Commander Stalin called me up and briefed me in general on a new operation being planned and the part my First Byelorussian Front was to play in it.

The front was to operate in the general direction of Bobruisk, Baranovichi, Warsaw, skirting Polesye in the north. The front's left wing abutted on the vast Polesye marshlands, which restricted the possibility of maneuvering to a bare minimum. The success of the operation required the closest coordination with the Second Byelorussian Front, from which we were separated by a large tract of wooded and marshy country. I outlined my views to Stalin, suggesting that it would be advisable to bring the whole zone occupied by both Byelorussian fronts under a single command.

Shortly afterward, a GHQ directive handed the whole Polesye sector with all forces in it over to our front. The total width of the zone of advance of the First Byelorussian Front thus reached almost 550 miles. Rarely in the last war was it usual for an army group on an offensive mission to occupy so great a frontage. Naturally, our forces increased accordingly, and by the latter half of June, the front included ten field armies, one tank and two air armies, the Dnieper River Flotilla, and, additionally, three tank, one mechanized, and three cavalry corps.

In an attempt to hold on to Byelorussia, the German Command concentrated large forces there: Army Group Center under Field Marshal von Busch (one tank and three field armies), several right-flank divisions of the 16th Army of Army Group North, and Panzer divisions of Army Group North Ukraine were also operating in the zone of our forthcoming offensive. Altogether in the front from Sirotino to Kovel there were, by June 23, 63 German divisions and 3 brigades with a total strength of 1,200,000. The enemy had 9,635 guns and mortars, 932 tanks, and 1,342 airplanes.

We prepared the campaign with great thoroughness. Planning was preceded by extensive work in the field, especially in the forward lines, where we often literally had to crawl about on all fours. After studying the terrain and drawing up a map of the enemy defenses, I decided that it would be worth dealing two strikes in different sectors of the front's right wing: one with the 3rd and 48th armies from Rogachov toward Bobruisk and Osipovichi, and the other with the 65th and 28th armies from the lower reaches of the Berezina and Ozarichi in the general direction of Slutsk. Both strikes were to be the main efforts. This ran contrary to established views, according to which there can be only one main attack, for which the main forces are assembled. This decision called for a certain dilution of forces, but it was deliberate: in the marshes of Polesye, there was no other way out—or, rather, there was no other way to achieve success in the operation.

The operation was code-named ''Bagration'' after the famous Russian military leader in the war against Napoleon in the early nineteenth century. The forces of the fronts were given important strategic and political objectives: to eliminate the enemy's salient in the Vitebsk-Bobruisk-Minsk area, to defeat and destroy Army Group Center, to liberate Byelorussia, and then to commence the liberation of Poland and subsequently carry the war to the territory of Nazi Germany. Great importance was attached to effective coordination, especially between the Third and First Byelorussian fronts, whose troops were to advance rapidly westward in a pincer movement that was to close west of Minsk.

Our front was to launch the offensive with four armies on the right flank, surround and annihilate the enemy's Bobruisk group, take the Bobruisk-Glusha-Glussk area, and then continue to advance toward Bobruisk-Minsk and Bobruisk-Baranovichi. The forces on the left wing were to advance after the German troops had been encircled in the neighborhood of Minsk and the right wing had reached the Baranovichi line.

The 3rd Army held a small bridgehead on the western bank of the Dnieper north of Rogachov that was quite suitable for action by all arms in the Bobruisk direction.

General Romanenko's 48th Army was much worse off. The army commander tried to attack the enemy from his positions.

I had crawled all over the frontline positions and seen that it was impossible to advance here. The surrounding terrain was one huge marsh dotted with small islands of shrubs and dense forest. There were no conditions for concentrating tanks and heavy artillery; a road for even a light gun would require several layers of logs. Therefore General Romanenko was ordered to regroup his main forces on the Rogachov bridgehead on the left flank of the 3rd Army and act jointly with it.

Our officers and men were faced with the extremely arduous task of fighting their way over this difficult terrain, a feat that required special training. Men learned to swim, cross swamps and rivers with any available means, and find their way through woods. They made special "swamp shoes" to cross the bogs, and built boats, rafts, and platforms for trundling machine guns, mortars, and light artillery. The tankmen also underwent training in the art of marsh warfare.

General Batov once showed me such a "tankodrome" in a marsh in the army rear. For more than an hour we watched machine after machine drive into the swamp and cross it to the other end. Helped by engineers, the crews provided each tank with branches, logs, and special triangles for crossing wide ditches. The engineers deserve special mention for their devoted work and resourcefulness. In 20 days in June they removed 34,000 enemy mines in the sector of the main attack, made 193 passages for tanks and infantry, and built dozens of crossings over the Drut and the Dnieper, to say nothing of building other types of roads.

Special attention was given to air, ground, and radio reconnaissance. The 16th Air Army carried out blanket aerial photography of the enemy's fortifications in the sector, and maps with the information obtained were circulated among the units. Our scouts took more than 80 information prisoners and many important documents.

All headquarters were required to maintain constant air and ground control over the effectiveness with which all activities at the front were concealed from the enemy. He was to see only what we wanted him to see. Troops deployed and regrouped under cover of night, while in the daytime trainloads of dummy tanks and guns traveled from the front to the rear. In many places we built fake crossings and roads. Guns were concentrated on secondary lines, from which they launched artillery attacks and were then removed to the rear, dummies being left in their place on the fire positions. Our Chief of Staff General Malinin was inexhaustibly inventive in this respect.

The observation posts were brought up as close to the troops as possible: distances from the line of departure were 500–1,000 yards for a divisional OP, a mile for a corps OP, up to 2 miles for an army OP. Observation towers were built in several places.

By the latter part of June, the front's troops were poised for the attack. On both strike sectors we had built up a three- to fourfold superiority over the enemy in manpower and a four- to sixfold superiority in artillery and armaments. We had powerful mobile groups capable of surrounding enemy troops, and air cover and support was to be provided by over 2,000 planes.

With the initiative completely in the hands of the Red Army and with an equal balance of forces on the scale of the front as a whole, we could even risk concentrating overwhelming forces on the main line of attack at the expense of weakening the secondary sectors substantially.

The First Byelorussian Front's offensive began on June 24, with powerful air strikes on both lines of attack. For two hours artillery pounded the enemy's defenses. At 6:00 A.M. troops of the 3rd and 48th armies went over to the offensive and an hour later it was followed by both armies of the southern strike force. Fierce fighting began.

During the first day, the 3rd Army achieved little success. In the face of fierce enemy infantry and Panzer counterattacks, two of its infantry corps succeeded in taking only the front-line and second-line trenches and were forced to dig in. The offensive on the 48th Army's sector also ran into difficulty. The wide marshy flood valley of the River Drut impeded the infantry and, especially, armor. It took two hours of severe fighting for our units to knock the Germans out of the front-line trenches, and the second line was captured by noon.

The offensive was most successful in the 65th Army's sector. In the first half of the day, the 18th Infantry Corps, supported by airplanes, broke through all five lines of enemy trenches and by midday had penetrated 3 to 4 miles, taking the powerful strongholds of Rakovichi and Petrovichi. This enabled General Batov to throw the 1st Guards Tank Corps into the breach, and it swiftly moved into the rear of the Germans.

Thus, in the first day, the southern strike group broke through the enemy defenses on a 20-mile frontage, penetrating 3 to 6 miles in depth. The tanks extended the breakthrough to a depth of 12 miles. This favorable situation was exploited on the second day by committing General Pliyev's combined cavalry and mechanized group to action at the junction of the 65th and 28th armies. It advanced to the River Ptich west of Glussk and forced the river at several points, whereupon the enemy began a general retreat to the north and northwest.

The time had now come to throw all forces into a swift advance on Bobruisk.

By the end of the third day, General Batov had reached

the Berezina River south of Bobruisk, while General
Luchinsky's troops had forced the River Ptich and taken
Glussk. The southern group of the front's right wing could
now take the offensive.

All during the night of June 24, the fighting continued
unabated on the front's northern wing. The enemy counterattacked repeatedly, striving to knock the wedge we had
driven into his defenses back into the river. This, however,
he was unable to do.

In the morning of June 25, after a brief artillery preparation, the 3rd Army resumed the offensive. In the middle of
the day, to accelerate the breakthrough, General Gorbatov
committed two tank brigades to action, and on June 26 the
9th Tank Corps was thrown in from the Dobritsa line with
the task of penetrating deep into the enemy's rear, capturing the Staritsa area and cutting off the Mogilev-Bobruisk
highway.

The 16th Air Army was ordered to support the northern
group's offensive. Thousands of tons of bombs were rained
on the enemy, who had begun to pull back to the Berezina.

The 9th Tank Corps broke into the enemy rear, reached
the eastern bank of the Berezina, and by the morning of
June 27, it had straddled all the highways and river crossings northeast of Bobruisk. The infantry units of both
armies of the northern group accelerated their advance,
enveloping the Bobruisk group from the northeast.

By this time, the 65th Army's 1st Guards Tank Corps
had made a thrust northwest of Bobruisk, cutting off five
German divisions from their westward retreat routes.

The front's main forces were to advance as far as possi-
ble. We also had to mop up the surrounded enemy forces.
In Bobruisk this task was assigned to units of the 65th
Army, and, southeast of the city, to the 48th Army.

About 40,000 Nazi troops were surrounded in a pocket
some 15 miles in diameter. We had sealed off their routes
of retreat to the south and west quite effectively, but on the
first day only isolated tank units held the surrounded en-

emy on the north and northwest. The commanding general of the German 9th Army decided to exploit this position, and on June 27 he ordered General von Lützow, Commander of the 35th Army Corps, to break through at all costs, either toward Bobruisk or northward toward Pogoreloye to join the 4th Army. Von Lützow decided to destroy all his materiel and strike northward. However, his plans failed.

Toward the evening of June 27, explosions and fires began in the enemy's dispositions as the Nazis destroyed guns, tractors, and tanks, burned machines, slaughtered cattle, and razed villages to the ground. Covering forces comprised of crack officers and men continued to resist stubbornly and occasionally even counterattacked. However, General Gorbatov's and General Romanenko's forces, in cooperation with units of the 65th Army, tightened the noose.

In two days the enemy lost more than 10,000 dead; we captured 6,000 prisoners, 432 guns, 250 mortars, and over 1,000 machine guns. This was the end of the Nazi group southeast of Bobruisk.

Meanwhile fighting continued for Bobruisk, where there were some 10,000 German soldiers, while remnants of scattered units were still making their way toward the city from the east. The commandant of Bobruisk organized a strong, thorough defense system, with weapon emplacements in buildings, barricades in the streets, and tanks dug into the ground on street corners. The approaches to the city were mined heavily.

In the afternoon of June 27, units of the 1st Guards Tank Corps and the 105th Infantry Corps attacked the enemy in the city, but failed to make any headway. Heavy fighting continued throughout the night and the following day. On the night of June 28, the enemy pulled back part of his troops to the city center and concentrated large forces of infantry and artillery in the northern and northwestern districts.

At dawn advance detachments of the 48th Army supported by artillery crossed the Berezina and engaged the enemy on the eastern outskirts of Bobruisk.

By 8:00 A.M. on June 29, regiments of the 354th Infantry Division took the railway station. The beleaguered Germans made one last-ditch attempt to break through to the northwest. They succeeded in penetrating our defenses, and 5,000 men headed by General Hofmeister, commander of the 41st Panzer Corps, poured into the breach. They did not get away, however, and our forces operating northwest of the city engaged and destroyed the fleeing enemy. On June 29, the 65th Army, jointly with the 48th Army, completed the liberation of Bobruisk.

In six days of fighting, we had captured or destroyed 366 tanks and self-propelled guns and 2,664 guns of different calibers. The enemy left nearly 50,000 dead on the battlefield, and more than 20,000 were captured.

On June 28, the GHQ gave the First Byelorussian Front the task of advancing on Minsk with some portion of its forces, while the main forces were to advance on Slutsk and Baranovichi, with the object of cutting off the enemy's lines of retreat to the southwest and then, jointly with troops of the Third Byelorussian Front, to effect a speedy encirclement of the enemy's Minsk group.

General Bakharov's tank corps, sent on a turning movement south of Minsk, captured the road junction of Lyubyach on July 2 and continued to advance northward along the Slutsk-Minsk highway. On the same day, tank units of the Third Byelorussian Front advanced on Minsk from the northeast, thus completing the encirclement of the enemy's 4th Army east of the Byelorussian capital.

Toward the end of July 3, after fierce fighting, the Byelorussian capital was completely cleared of the enemy.

The mopping up of the Nazi troops in the Minsk pocket was assigned to the Second Byelorussian Front, reinforced by the 3rd Army taken from us.

Troops of the First Byelorussian Front's right wing con-

tinued their swift westward advance. The defeat of the
enemy at Vitebsk, Bobruisk, and east of Minsk resulted in
a 250-mile breach in the German front which the Nazi
Command could not fill. The GHQ demanded that we
make all possible use of this favorable situation. It was
decided to continue to pursue the enemy and, by a pincer
movement of the 48th and 65th armies in the general
direction of Baranovichi, surround the Baranovichi group
and destroy it. General Pliyev's mobile group and General
Firsovich's mechanized corps, operating on the flanks,
were to envelop the enemy. Then both armies would continue toward Brest to envelop and surround the German
Pinsk group, jointly with units of our left wing.

On July 8 Baranovichi was liberated, and by July 16 our
formations advanced 95–105 miles in twelve days.

The time had come to move the troops on our left wing
forward; we had five field armies, an air army, a tank
army, and two cavalry corps. Early in July we began
regrouping to transfer the front's reinforcements from the
right wing to the left.

The battalions began the attack. With a small group of
generals, I occupied a forward observation post which
offered a good view of the battlefield. Supported by strong
artillery fire and accompanied by tanks, they advanced
quickly toward the enemy positions. The Germans replied
with powerful artillery fire. Small groups of our aircraft
attacked artillery and mortar positions. They were met in
the air by enemy fighters. Gradually the enemy committed
more and more guns to action.

In some places our infantrymen and individual tanks
broke into the forward trenches. The pitch of the fighting
rose higher and higher. There seemed to be no doubt that
we were up against the main line of defense. There was no
purpose in waiting any longer, so I ordered the troops to
proceed with the full offensive plan.

General Kazakov ordered the artillery to open fire, and
the roar of guns of all calibers shook the air.

On the morning of July 18, our units broke through the
enemy defenses on a 20-mile front and advanced 8 miles;
and on July 20, the strike groups on the left flank reached
the Western Bug River, forced it at three points, and
entered Poland.

The July fighting in the First Byelorussian Front's left
wing, together with the offensive launched a week earlier
by the First Ukrainian Front, our neighbor to the left,
developed into a well-coordinated campaign of two fronts
operating on adjacent flanks. Our success was greatly
facilitated because the First Ukrainian Front's offensive
had prevented the enemy from reinforcing his troops on
the Lublin sector; reciprocally, our attacks prevented him
from transferring troops against the First Ukrainian Front.

The Red Army's powerful July offensive, which had
involved five fronts, resulted in the rout of the German
Army Groups North (16th Army), Center (4th, 9th, 2nd,
and 3rd Panzer armies) and North Ukraine (4th and 1st
Panzer armies and the Hungarian 1st Army). The enemy's
defenses were breached along a huge frontage.

At last the time had come when the enemy, who had
unleashed the war, began to experience what the Red
Army had experienced in the beginning. There was a
difference, though, for we had weathered our setbacks in
the knowledge that to a great extent they had been due to
the suddenness of the enemy's treacherous attack. We had
known they were temporary and had never lost faith in the
ultimate victorious outcome of the war. The enemy's defeats came after all the victories he had achieved, leaving
him no hope for a more or less favorable outcome of the
war whose flames he had kindled himself.

Our front's right wing reached the approaches to Brest,
setting the stage for envelopment of the enemy's Brest
grouping. This task was assigned to the 70th and 28th
armies.

The 47th Army was ordered to force the River Bug,
advance to the southwest on Siedlce, defeat the opposition,

and prevent any German forces deployed east of the Siedlce-Lukow line from pulling back to Warsaw. Also fighting on this sector was General Kryukov's 2nd Guards Cavalry Corps.

The advance of these armies contributed to the success of those led by Chuikov, Bogdanov, Berling, and Kolpakchi, who were racing westward after crossing the Bug. Overcoming enemy resistance, they captured Chelm and Wlodawa and liberated many other communities.

On July 23, the 2nd Tank Army liberated Lublin, and on July 25 it reached the Vistula at Deblin. Here General Radzievsky, who had replaced the wounded Bogdanov, handed his sector over to the Polish 1st Army advancing in the tank army's wake. The tanks were given the new task of thrusting northward along the right bank of the Vistula, taking the Warsaw suburb of Praga in their stride and holding it until the approach of the 47th Army. The Polish 1st Army was to force the Vistula on the Deblin sector and establish a bridgehead on the western bank.

By July 28, having encountered stubborn resistance, the front's main forces were compelled to deploy their front line facing north. The German Command had concentrated large forces in this sector, obviously with the intention of delivering a southward counterblow east of the Vistula, to prevent our armies from crossing the river.

The enemy's main grouping was concentrated east of Warsaw, and the units on the front's left wing were therefore able to advance rapidly toward the Vistula. General Kolpakchi's 69th Army reached the river, went straight over it, and seized a bridgehead on the western bank. The Polish 1st Army made an unsuccessful attempt to strike across the Vistula. By this time, though, we could throw the whole of the 8th Guards Army into the fight for the western bank, and, on the morning of August 1, this army began to force the river.

During the course of the day, General Chuikov's troops established a bridgehead on the western bank 10 miles wide and up to 6 miles deep. The army had thrown several 16-ton pontoon bridges and one 60-ton bridge over the river. Chuikov used them to take his armor and all of his artillery over to the bridgehead. Then the engineers built a wooden bridge on piles.

The troops of the Second Byelorussian Front on our right were advancing very slowly on Bialystok. They had a very powerful enemy group before them. But though the enemy was capable of withstanding their attacks, he was unable to strike at our front's right wing, thanks to the Second Byelorussian Front; we appreciated their help greatly.

By the time the enemy realized the danger facing him, it was too late: the bridgehead was held firmly by the units of the 8th Guards Army, and the bridgehead south of Pulawy was equally firmly held by the 69th Army. The German Command began to transfer troops from sectors east and northeast of Warsaw to attack the bridgeheads.

Information provided by intelligence, air, and radio reconnaissance confirmed the hasty transfer of enemy troops to the Magnoszew bridgehead. Chuikov's Guards needed help. We appealed to our comrades-in-arms, the Poles. Handing over the line along the Vistula bank to a cavalry corps, the Polish army rushed to the bridgehead, where it took up defensive positions on the 8th Guards Army's right flank. At the same time we managed to ferry over a tank corps of the 2nd Tank Army.

We were just in time. The enemy struck a powerful blow at the bridgehead. It was too late! Our defense proved invincible. Several days of fierce attacks yielded nothing for the Nazis but tremendous losses.

The friendship of Soviet and Polish units was cemented in the course of the heavy fighting. The men of the Polish 1st Army fought bravely against the Nazi invaders and won well-deserved respect.

We could now look back with deep satisfaction on Operation Bagration, carried out so brilliantly by our several fronts under overall GHQ guidance. As a result, Army

Group Center had been been routed completely, Army
Group North Ukraine had suffered a major defeat, while
Byelorussia, a large part of Latvia, and substantial areas of
Poland east of the Vistula had been liberated. Soviet troops
had forged the rivers Nieman and Narew and reached the
borders of East Prussia. The way to Germany was open.

9. The Liberation of the Crimea

Marshal of the Soviet Union Sergei Biryuzov (1904–1964) was in army service since 1922. At the beginning of the Second World War, he was a division commander and later an army chief of staff of a front from the spring of 1943. After the war, he commanded the forces of several military districts, was a Deputy Defense Minister, then Commander-in-Chief of the Strategic Missile Forces, and later Chief of the General Staff of the Soviet Armed Forces.

During the events described below, he was Chief of Staff of the Fourth Ukrainian Front.

The spring of 1944 was coming into its own, enveloping the whole country as it moved farther and farther north. And, as if to meet it, the Soviet Army extended its offensive from the ice-covered shores of the Gulf of Finland toward the south, taking over the initiative at more and more fronts. In January the forces of the Leningrad Front finally broke the enemy blockade of the city, and in coordination with the Volkhov and Second Baltic fronts, smashed a large grouping of the Nazi Army. The second crushing blow was dealt at the enemy in the Right-Bank

Ukraine between February and April. And the third blow was being prepared in the Crimea.

Hitler attached enormous political importance to holding the Crimean Peninsula. The presence of a strong Nazi force there exerted certain influence on the position of Turkey and also on Germany's allies, Romania and Bulgaria. Besides, by clinging on to the Crimea, the enemy blocked the operations of our Black Sea Fleet.

The forces of the Fourth Ukrainian Front were assigned the key role in the Crimean operation. The Separate Maritime Army, which was to deliver an auxiliary blow from Kerch, was to be incorporated in our front after reaching the Crimean's central areas. From the sea, the operation was to be supported by the ships and marines of the Black Sea Fleet, the Azov Flotilla. In the enemy's rear, we were helped by the Crimean guerrillas, who were quite numerous by that time.

In accordance with the plan, the Fourth Ukrainian Front and the Separate Maritime Army were to deliver converging blows on Sevastopol from the north and east. That would cut the Nazi force in two and make it easier to destroy it altogether. The Black Sea Fleet was to blockade the enemy and destroy enemy ships which might try to evacuate Nazi troops from the Crimea.

Preparations were made in secrecy. The enemy never did learn in what sector we were going to deliver the main blow: across Perekop or from the Sivash bridgehead. The staffs and army engineers had done a great deal to mislead the enemy as to our true intentions, and with great success. The Nazis failed to determine the hour or even the day of our attack.

Guns boomed for several successive days on the Perekop isthmus, where the positions were held by the 2nd Guards Army commanded by Lieutenant-General Zakharov. Its artillery was destroying enemy fortifications. According to POWs, the Nazis were especially stunned by the performance of our heavy guns. Their bulky 660-pound shells literally wiped enemy bunkers off the surface of the earth in direct hits.

To divert the enemy's attention from the main direction of attack, a large grouping of our troops disembarked southwest of Melitopol and created the impression of moving southward. We set up dummy concentration areas of four rifle divisions near Genichesk and other regions.

Although the Nazis observed strict camouflage, we possessed exhaustive information about the location of their fire emplacements and the system of fortifications.

Information about the enemy came to us through many channels: it was gathered by pilots who photographed the location of enemy troops, by radio operators who intercepted every word dropped indiscreetly by Nazi commanders, and by our scouts wearing camouflage suits, whose feats had become legend and who did their dangerous job under the very nose of the enemy. We could have formed a whole unit out of the prisoners they had captured and brought with them across enemy lines.

So what was the enemy force facing us?

The Germans had two defense zones on the Perekop isthmus 20 to 22 miles deep. Barbed-wire entanglements were set up, and minefields laid all along the forward line of defense. They were defended by the 50th Infantry Division, the Bergmann Regiment, four separate infantry battalions, two engineer battalions, and many special units. Their total strength was 20,000.

The defense of Sivash was somewhat different. It was based on several commanding heights separated by lakes and inlets into sections. Each of these made up a sector of the front, as it were. The sections maintained fire liaison, and the enemy defense there also consisted of two—and, in some places, three—zones manned chiefly by Romanian forces.

The 5th Nazi Army Corps was in the Kerch peninsula. Two Romanian divisions and some of the special German units were guarding the rest of the Crimean coast and

doing garrison duty in the cities. The total strength of the
enemy troops in the Crimea reached 200,000.

Finally April 8 came.

The forces at the front launched the offensive at 10:30
A.M. after a powerful artillery preparation and massive
bombardment. The 51st Army delivered the main blow
from the bridgehead on the southern coast of Sivash.
Incidentally, it was the same army which, together with
other units, fought bitter battles in 1941 in an attempt to
block the enemy's advance to the Crimea.

The assault on the enemy fortifications in the Perekop
isthmus began at the same time. The offensive there was
mounted by the units of the 2nd Guards Army supported
by considerable artillery forces.

By that time, we had introduced a number of innova-
tions in the use of artillery, having to do with feigned
shifts of fire. It is worth going into the history of this
tactic.

During the many days of "boring into" the enemy
defenses on the River Molochnaya, we had observed that
our infantry often failed to capture enemy trenches. Thousands of shells would rain on those trenches during the
artillery preparation, and it seemed that no one in the
trenches would survive. But when fire was shifted deeper
into the enemy defenses and infantrymen dashed to the
forward positions, they would come under machine-gun
fire 50 to 60 yards from them.

It was the enemy who helped us to find out at last how
his fire emplacements managed to survive. A captured
German officer told us that during our artillery preparation, the whole company took shelter in deep dugouts.
Only eight or ten submachine gunners stayed in the
trenches. Their task was simple: to open fire on the attackers immediately after the artillery preparation. Under this fire cover,
the Nazis would leave their dugouts, get back to the
trenches, and put up organized resistance to our infantry.

As a countermeasure, we decided to carry out feigned

artillery maneuvers. At the end of the artillery preparation, half of the guns and mortars would shift fire deep into the enemy defenses while the other half would suddenly stop firing. The infantry put out dummies to create the impression that soldiers were rising to attack. The Nazis would come out of their shelters, and at that moment the silent artillery would again start pounding the forward trenches. That pattern was repeated several times.

Within the first hour, the left-flank regiment of the 347th Rifle Division moving under the cover of a smoke screen managed to reach a height one-half mile north of Kula. Toward the evening, the Nazis had been pushed back all along the central sector and had been dislodged from the heavily fortified strongpoint of Armyansk. The bridgehead south of the Turkish Rampart had been widened and the enemy forces to the right and left of it faced the real danger of encirclement.

The enemy put up unusually stiff resistance, making skillful use of the terrain favorable for defense. However, at night, the first echelon regiments of the 267th Rifle Division, which was part of the 63rd Rifle Corps, crossed the barbed-wire lines and burst into the third trench.

At dawn fighting flared up with renewed force. A battalion of the 267th Rifle Division that had advanced was cut off from the rest of our troops, but continued to hold the captured positions and beat off enemy counterattacks. A regiment of the neighboring 346th Rifle Division came to its help under heavy artillery cover.

The enemy held on to the Turkish Rampart with tenacity. Our thorough preliminary artillery and air preparation did not save us from oncoming fire assaults. Many enemy pillboxes were not destroyed.

Some of the trenches changed hands several times. In a number of places, our guards units had to resort to trickery. They put dummies wearing army tunics and helmets out of the trenches to create the impression of an attack. Visual deception was backed by yelling of "Hurrahs."

And the Nazis would fall for the bait. When they emerged hurriedly from their shelters and foxholes to take up their positions in the trenches, our artillery resumed firing.

The trick was repeated several times. Only after substantial enemy forces had been wiped out and the enemy had ceased to react to the manipulations with the dummies did our guards battalions rise to a real attack.

The Separate Maritime Army commanded by General Yeremenko began to advance the following day. The Black Sea Fleet had also stepped up its activity. The Nazi defenses in the Crimea began to crumble.

The offensive by the forces of the Fourth Ukrainian Front continued to develop. The 417th Rifle Division—the second echelon of 63rd Rifle Corps—was committed to action from the direction of the Sivash bridgehead. The 32nd Guards Tank Brigade and several artillery regiments and guards mortar units were also moved there.

At dawn on April 11 we brought reinforcements—the 19th Tank Corps and the 77th Rifle Division—into the breach. By noon they had captured Dzhankoi, a major rail and road junction in the northern part of the Crimea which had served as a base for logistical supplies for a considerable part of the German forces. From Dzhankoi we could now proceed to Simferopol.

The front commander ordered the formation of a mobile group to speed up the liberation of that biggest city in the Crimea and the regional center where the HQ of the 17th German Army and the 49th Alpine Rifle Corps were then situated. The mobile group included the 19th Tank Corps, the 279th Motorborne Rifle Division, and the 21st Antitank Artillery Brigade.

The 2nd Guards Army would pursue the enemy as he pulled back to Sevastopol. Two of its divisions headed for Yevpatoria, and one advanced along the seacoast.

The whole of the southwestern coast of the Crimean peninsula had been cleared of the invaders by the evening of April 13. The commander of the front's artillery and I were with the 19th Tank Corps, where we watched a moving scene: the liberation of Simferopol.

We rode into the city when it was still enveloped in gunpowder smoke. The final battle was fought on the southern and eastern outskirts. Some of the houses and even whole blocks were destroyed, but on the whole the city had managed to survive. The swift advance of the Soviet forces prevented the enemy from carrying out its savage schemes of destroying all housing, cultural facilities, parks, and gardens. The city looked beautiful in its springtime attire of greenery and flowers.

The Separate Maritime Army was already moving toward linking up with the forces of our front. Our air-force units gave considerable assistance to its advance. On April 11 air-reconnaissance soldiers spotted the beginning of the enemy's retreat from the Kerch peninsula. His attempt to break away from the Separate Maritime Army—or, to put it simply, to give it the slip—failed. Our left-flank neighbor immediately began to pursue the enemy troops.

The Separate Maritime Army linked up with us on April 18 and was incorporated into the Fourth Ukrainian Front. Later, operating together with the 51st Army, it played a prominent role in the liberation of the Crimea's southern coast.

The 2nd Guards Army was the first to reach Sevastopol from the north and northeast. The Separate Maritime Army, having driven the enemy out of Balaklava, started fighting on the eastern and southeastern slopes of Mt. Sapun.

Thus the whole of the Crimea, except for the Sevastopol fortified area, had been cleared of the enemy. It was a great victory. But we failed to burst into the city on the heels of the retreating enemy and free Sevastopol from march column.

In general, it is difficult to capture a fortified area from march column. Had we had airborne troops at that time, we might have managed it; but we had none. Moreover,

even our bombers and attack planes could not support our
rifle and tank units when they approached the outer ring of
the defense line at Sevastopol.

The taking of Sevastopol required painstaking preparation. Not only had the Nazis rebuilt the permanent reinforced concrete fortifications the Soviet forces put up in
1941 and 1942, but the enemy had strengthened them in
every possible way. The enemy had tremendous firepower:
32 machine guns and 15 mortars for every Soviet rifle
company in the first wave. The Nazi Command had concentrated about 72,000 officers and men in the small patch
of land near Sevastopol.

In all, the Soviet divisions' assault groups were re-
formed to move ahead of the infantry combat formations
and destroy pillboxes, machine-gun emplacements, and
other obstacles. The groups underwent special training on
the terrain in order to master the techniques of destroying
fire emplacements in the mountains and fighting in trenches.

After hearing a detailed report from the chief of reconnaissance and myself, the front's military council, together
with representatives from GHQ, adopted a final plan for
the completion of the Crimean operation. We would deliver the main attack from the east and southeast of the
city.

It was a soft and clear morning in the Crimea on May 5,
1944. Suddenly the earth began to tremble, and rolling
peals of thunder echoed in the mountain valleys. Black
clouds of smoke and dust rose over Sevastopol.

For two hours our artillery and air-force units pounded
the Nazi defense fortifications. The rate of fire increased
with every minute. It was impossible to talk, and we had
to communicate with each other by gestures. In the final
ten minutes of the fire assault, the air itself seemed to be
taut when guards' mortar units joined in.

Even when the troops began their assault, the artillery
continued firing. The assault was exceptionally rapid and

successful. The guardsmen forged ahead, climbing the slopes of the Mekenziyev Hills.

The enemy had no doubt that it was there that the main attack was launched, and immediately began to bring up infantry and artillery units from other sectors. That was all we needed.

Long before daybreak soldiers of the 12th Assault Engineer Brigade had cleared ten 15-yard passages in the numerous rows of the enemy's barbed-wire entanglements. They had also cleared passages in the minefields. It was those difficult preparations, carried out with some loss of life, that enabled the 77th Rifle Division to reach the first line of enemy trenches in a matter of minutes.

The Soviet forces assumed the offensive all along the front on the morning of May 7. And everywhere they ran into stiff enemy resistance.

Mt. Sapun was clearly visible from the observation post of General Koshevoi, Commander of the 63rd Rifle Corps. It was enveloped in smoke and dust. The Nazis came out of their shelters time and again in a bid to counterattack our units. Fierce hand-to-hand fighting broke out.

Night was already falling when the first red flags appeared on the crest of the mountain in the zone of attack of the 51st Army. The advance units of the 11th Guards Rifle Corps of the Separate Maritime Army reached the mountain and Karagach Hill a little to the south almost at the same time.

During the battles, I witnessed a rather curious spectacle: a long file of Soviet soldiers carrying some big black boxes toward the shore. After looking more closely at them, we saw that those were coffins with white Nazi swastikas painted on their sides. I was wondering where the men were carrying them. Only when the soldiers began to lower the coffins onto the water and sit on them to cross the harbor on those improvised rafts did everything become clear. Nazi logistics officers had out of "concern" for the garrison defending Sevastopol provided it with a large number of coffins well in advance. However, the enemy could not use even them. Our units, having driven the Nazis from the shore of the Northern Bay, captured their funeral storehouse. Without wasting time in search of more suitable material, the Soviet soldiers used the products of the German undertakers for their crossing.

Fighting had moved to the city streets. Units of the 51st Army had burst through the enemy defenses in the northeastern and eastern outskirts. The Separate Maritime Army was advancing on Sevastopol from the southwest. The 19th Tank Corps was forging ahead successfully in the coastal area. Marine brigades fought side by side with the troops of the Fourth Ukrainian Front.

There still remained a rather large enemy force in the Crimea. It had been pushed to the shore in Cape Khersones, where it fought back ferociously while waiting for a convoy of ships from Romania to evacuate them.

On the night of May 12 we brought up large artillery units and conducted powerful air preparation. At daybreak, units of the Separate Maritime Army as well as the 10th Rifle Corps of the 51st Army launched their attack. This time the enemy could not put up any serious resistance. Evidently the Nazis had been demoralized.

Shortly afterward, Commander of the Tenth Corps Major-General Neverov reported that his regiments had reached the seashore, where they saw countless numbers of killed enemy officers and men.

"Where did they come from?" I asked in surprise. "There has been no real fighting yet." A liaison officer who drove up at that moment confirmed that he had seen "heaps of corpses."

The mystery was solved by General Neverov himself. When he came close to the "countless corpses," he discovered that those lying on the ground were live enemy officers and men who pretended to be dead. After our tanks had passed, they jumped up quickly and stood before our infantry, raising their hands in surrender.

By midday on May 12, there was not a single armed enemy soldier left in the Crimea. The remains of the 17th German Army were taken prisoner. The enemy had lost over 111,000 men killed or taken prisoner in the battle for the peninsula. The 17th German Army and the Romanian divisions had also lost all of their weaponry. The enemy air force and navy sustained heavy losses, too.

The rout of the enemy grouping in the Crimea changed the situation on the Black Sea radically in our favor. The Soviet Black Sea Fleet and Air Force were able to operate on the enemy supply routes more effectively. The Nazi Command, on the other hand, having lost Sevastopol, could use only the ports in Romania and Bulgaria. The Turkish government revised its foreign policy and refused flatly to take armed action against the Soviet Union.

10. Toward the Balkans

*Marshal of the Soviet Union Rodion Malinovsky (1898–1967)
joined the army in 1914. During the First World War, he was
a private in the Russian Expeditionary Corps in France. He
began the Second World War as a commander of the rifle
corps, then commanded an army. He commanded a number
of fronts from 1943 until the end of the war. After the war, he
was in command of several military districts and was the
Commander-in-Chief of the Ground Forces and Minister of
Defense of the USSR.*

In April 1944 the troops of the Second Ukrainian Front
under Marshal Konev conducted a successful offensive
in the Ukraine on the right bank of the Dnieper and entered
Romanian territory. They continued the offensive in order
to capture Jassy and the adjoining area and then to exploit
the offensive to the oil-rich parts of Romania. But they
were unable to fulfill their mission.

In accordance with a decision by General Headquarters,
I handed over command of the Third Ukrainian Front to
General of the Army Tolbukhin and assumed command of
the troops of the Second Ukrainian Front. Marshal Konev,

in turn, took over command of the First Ukrainian Front in place of Marshal Zhukov who began to fulfill his main duty at that time: that of Deputy Supreme Commander.

I reached the troops of the Second Ukrainian Front at a time when the fighting between Targu-Frumos and Jassy, far from petering out, became very heavy at times.

The enemy was not content merely with holding back the advance of the troops of the Second Ukrainian Front at this line. He mounted determined counterblows in late May and early June in an attempt to push us back to the valley of the River Prut. We had to act decisively to ward off these counterblows and strengthen the 27th Army with tanks from the 2nd Tank Army and the 52nd Army with tanks from the 6th Tank Army.

These enemy blows were quite heavy. From the 52nd Army, which was holding the front before Jassy, often came disturbing reports, such as the loss of one or two trenches, or a whole position; a hill or even a group of hills. There was a threat of our losing hills in the Jassy area which would cause great harm to our position. Fortunately, we had enough strength to strike a decisive blow at the enemy to force him to stop his activities.

It did not seem much of a problem. We could advance a couple of divisions or a corps and strike at the enemy to weaken his resolve. Proposals to this effect were made both at the Front Headquarters and by individual commanders. But I had no wish to take this course of action. I did not intend to use the hills before Jassy as the starting position for a new offensive operation, but they had to be held at all costs to make the enemy believe that we *would* start our offensive from these particular hills.

I held a similar attitude about bridgeheads which we held beyond water obstacles. I did not always consider them as a base from which new operations should be carried out, but would rather use them to divert the enemy's attention and do everything necessary to convince him that the new operation would begin from these particular bridgeheads. I always considered it more expedient to prepare and carry out such an operation in a new direction. As a matter of fact, the enemy was often fooled by this ruse, so I decided to use the same tactics here.

No one knew my plans for using the hills near Jassy. I was advised insistently to "hold down" the enemy so as not to lose these hills. I decided to consult Supreme Commander-in-Chief Stalin on this matter.

I telephoned him and reported, "The situation is such that it would seem necessary to hold down the Germans. They are making persistent counterattacks, while the unstable position of the 52nd Army makes me apprehensive that our troops are really in danger of losing the hills in the Jassy area, which would put me at a disadvantage. Therefore I am ready to launch a strong attack against the enemy and ask permission to use a couple of divisions from the front reserve in order to reinforce the 52nd Army and kill any desire the enemy might have to counterattack us."

Stalin thought and said, "I don't recommend it."

"Why? We have plenty of reserves."

"That is exactly why I don't recommend it," he answered. "You know that as soon as you bring one or two divisions into action in this direction, the enemy will also bring up reinforcements in this direction. Then you will bring in more troops, and protracted fighting will start, which is not in our interests. So I don't recommend it and can't allow you to bring in front reserves in this direction."

I began to understand the Supreme Commander-in-Chief's line of thought. "I fully understand and shall act accordingly."

"And besides," Stalin said, "we shall now be taking troops from you for another direction, where we are preparing a new offensive operation."

So it was. Soon we dispatched the 5th Guards Field Army, two tank armies, and several more divisions to the General Headquarters Reserve.

Thus the enemy had been active constantly at Jassy

while we were pulling out troops from that direction. The enemy had come to the conclusion that the front was being weakened, to the extent that we had no strength to respond to his fire in equal measure, that we were throwing all our last efforts into holding the hills near Jassy. This was of great advantage to us because the enemy had been misled.

After several armies and corps had been taken away from us, the front and the armies still retained substantial reserves. The front included six field armies, and the front reserve had a tank army, and two tanks, one motorized, and one Cossack corps. But the enemy thought we had been weakened, so in June he began boldly to dispatch reserves from Army Group Southern Ukraine to the Byelorussian direction, where the situation for him was becoming grave.

Everything was quiet: we did not attack the enemy and he did not attack us. It was essential that the enemy believe the Second Ukrainian Front to be weak. There is no need to mention the Third Ukrainian Front, which had also been weakened seriously. For instance, it had been deprived of a guards army and tank and artillery units which had been transferred to the GHQ Reserve.

While preparing for the Jassy-Kishinev operation, we reinforced our divisions from the front's inner resources and with new replacements. We were able to make good what we lacked in equipment, tanks, self-propelled guns, artillery pieces, mortars, and other weapons. We also stocked shells and aviation fuel, regrouped some of our forces, carried out related measures, mapped out future routes for transport columns and crossings, and built underwater bridges across rivers.

There is much to be said for these underwater bridges, especially in muddy rivers. Enemy aircraft could not spot them easily, but of course they would eventually; so surface bridges had to be built as well to distract the enemy's attention.

We succeeded in doing all this secretly. The enemy was unaware of the regrouping.

For division commanders advancing in the first wave, large-scale relief maps were made showing divisional demarcation lines. These maps helped division and regiment commanders to study carefully every tiny hillock, gully, position, and trench, every center of the enemy's defense, and thoroughly work out a plan for attacking his positions.

Commanders of armies, corps, divisions, regiments, including myself as the front commander, held briefings with our subordinates to ascertain how and from where to attack the enemy, where the main blow had to be struck, and with what forces and equipment, how much fire should be concentrated on the enemy's key defensive positions, and at what time and at what intervals to attack in order to overwhelm the enemy completely. We worked out in detail how many tanks and self-propelled guns each division would have to support the infantry.

We had enough artillery. Initially we planned to break through at the front of 14 miles. In this particular area we were able to concentrate up to 350 guns per mile with a caliber of 76 mm and higher. When I reported the plan of operations at the GHQ Stalin said that this number was insufficient, that more guns were required. I answered that no more were available. He then proposed to attack on a 10-, not 14-mile, front. As a result, we had a density of 400–415 guns per mile of the front. On the main direction of attack the density was even higher, up to 450 guns per mile.

We had the 6th Tank Army, which comprised two corps, a self-propelled gun brigade, a heavy tank regiment, and other units. We also had the 18th Tank Corps. All these troops were meant to ensure a successful operation. We did not know how the situation would develop and wondered whether we would be able to bring them into the breakthrough on the first or second day of the offensive. War is a complex affair where it is necessary to work out as much as possible in advance and where one must be ready for everything. So we put the 6th Tank Army into the assault position, dug in the machines so that they could be neither seen nor heard; but at the same time, they were ready to start moving as soon as the signal was given.

The operation began at dawn on August 20. All commanders, including myself, were at the forward observation posts. There were artillerymen, tankmen, and airmen there. Some 400 yards ahead were the army commanders' advanced observation posts. Corps commanders were naturally stationed still closer to the front line. The observation posts protected the leading commanders from enemy fire.

The enemy was so taken by surprise by the artillery preparation that our tankmen and infantry had little difficulty breaking through his defensive positions and began successfully to mount an offensive. Only sporadic fire was returned by the enemy's individual guns and batteries.

Engineers carrying bridge sections followed the infantry and tanks into the swampy valley. About midnight on August 20, the commander of the engineering troops reported to me that the bridges were ready. During the day, the 6th Tank Army entered the breach, which took the enemy completely by surprise.

Our tankmen advanced steadily. The first day was a major success. The next day, the 18th Tank Corps was brought into action. On the same day, we took the town of Jassy and captured the mountain ridge of Mare, which is beyond Jassy. After that the operation began to advance. Our infantry, particularly the 3rd Guards Rifle Division, following close after the tank army, marched up to 30 miles a day. The tankmen found it awkward not to be able to break away from the division, so they forged ahead with more enthusiasm. This enabled the operation to proceed more rapidly.

After this decisive blow, the Romanian troops considered all resistance pointless and surrendered. This was not the case with the Germans, who continued to hit back hard.

A few words about the qualities of the Romanian soldier. We know that the Romanian army in the late war had rather low combat qualities, which was natural for soldiers fighting for a cause that was alien to them. But generally the Romanians were capable of great courage and valor, as I saw when Romanian and Soviet troops fought against the Germans. Some Romanian divisions drew our admiration by their fighting spirit, courage, and self-sacrifice.

I received the GHQ's order to lead the 4th Guards Army onto the western bank of the Prut. It was engaged in heavy fighting and had difficulty in breaking away from the enemy, yet we managed to disengage the army and move it to the river's right bank. At the same time, the enemy broke through from the "Kishinev pocket," also onto the Prut's right bank. The 52nd Army, which was advancing in the first echelon, found itself in a grave situation with a large number of German troops in its rear. Since tens of thousands of the Germans had broken out of the "Kishinev pocket," as well as their tanks, self-propelled guns, and artillery, we had to fight in the rear of the front.

Luckily we had troops to spare. The front had in its reserve two infantry corps and the 4th Guards Army, which was free now that it had reached the right bank of the Prut. These reserves helped us out of our difficulty.

I would like to say a few words about the significance of the moral factor in combat. In 1941 I happened to see men from rear units, who seldom had met the enemy face-to-face and were ill-prepared for independent fighting, scatter at the sight of a few German motorcyclists. I also saw our people fighting the Germans who had broken into our rear during the Jassy-Kishinev operation. This was true heroism. I admired the way our drivers and artillerymen fought without any help from the infantry. They fought the enemy courageously, repulsed his attacks, and made sure that not a single German escaped.

We had eliminated the enemy troops which had broken into our front, but it cost us a good deal in time and additional difficulties. Should the 4th Guards Army have continued operating on the Prut's eastern bank, it would have prevented the breakthrough of the surrounded enemy, or, in any case, would have tied up a considerable number of his troops and restricted his movements into our rear.

What was the outcome of the operation? By the way of an answer, I would like to relate the following episode. Soon after the operation began, Stalin, wishing to help our front in some way, offered us a group of mechanized cavalry commanded by General Pliyev. ''It will be useful when you fight for Galatz,'' Stalin said.

I replied that I would accept it with pleasure, for I knew General Pliyev as an excellent commander under whom the troops always fought well. But the mechanized group joined the front only when we were already crossing the Transylvanian Alps.

This shows the rapid advancement of the offensive, which is the main outcome of the operation that quickly and decisively changed the political and strategic situation in the Balkans and on the left wing of the entire Soviet-German front in general.

As a result of the Jassy-Kishinev operation, Army Group Southern Ukraine was completely routed, and 22 German divisions were wiped out. This created a favorable situation for an armed antifascist uprising by the Romanian people. Romania ceased to be Nazi Germany's ally and declared war on the fascists. The road to the Balkans and neighboring Bulgaria, Yugoslavia, Czechoslovakia, and Hungary was now open to the Soviet Union.

11. Breakthrough to the Baltic

Marshal of the Soviet Union Ivan Bagramyan (1897–1982) entered military service in 1915. During the Second World War, was the chief of staff of a front, the commander of an army, and the commander of several fronts. After the war, commanded a military district, was the Commander of the Academy of the General Staff, Deputy Minister of Defense, and Inspector General of the Ministry of Defense of the USSR.

In the summer of 1944, I commanded the troops of the First Baltic Front. Early in July the advanced units of our front approached the borders of Latvia and Lithuania, while some mobile detachments had already set foot on Lithuanian soil. We were convinced that the enemy would hold the Baltic region to the last. With this aim in view, he had set up a fortified complex defense manned by strong forces. It was only at the junction of Army Groups North and Center that the position of the Nazi troops was less secure. It was here that we stood against the thoroughly exhausted formations of the 3rd Panzer Army. This was a favorable opportunity for us to advance our offensive still farther. By driving deep wedges by the front's main forces toward Daugavpils (Dvinsk) and Švenčionys, we would have a genuine chance first of surrounding the right wing of Army Group North from the south, and then, by a decisive thrust into Riga, of cutting that city off from East Prussia.

On the night of July 4 we received the following directive: "The First Baltic Front to deliver the main blow in the general direction of Švenčionys—Kaunas—with the forces of the 2nd, 6th Guards, 39th, 43rd, and 51st armies."

We realized that the General Headquarters intended a further encirclement of the southern wing of Army Group North by our front and strikes from the other Baltic fronts from the northeast to force the enemy to retreat from Estonia and Latvia and to East Prussia. For this reason it was desirable that the troops of the First Baltic Front intercept his retreat.

After appraising the situation, we decided to rout the Daugavpils and Švenčionys enemy groupings with the troops of the 6th Guards and 43rd armies and the 1st Tank Corps in conjunction with the 4th Strike Army of the Second Baltic Front and the troops of the right wing of the Third Byelorussian Front and reach the Daugavpils-Pabrade railway. This would make conditions favorable for bringing in the 39th Army on the southern wing of the front.

Generals Chistyakov and Beloborodov redeployed their troops and set up strike forces during the fighting. Their armies continued fighting toward the west. The troops of the 6th Guards Army advanced somewhat more slowly because their formations were spread over a nearly 100-mile front. Not only were they unable to support the neighboring troops advancing toward Kaunas, but they were themselves barely able to oppose the mounting resistance of the Daugavpils enemy grouping. Despite their long front, Chistyakov's guardsmen advanced 30 miles between July 5 and July 12. To the left of the 6th Guards Army, the troops of the 43rd Army under General Beloborodov, a skillful and persistent commander, were operating on a broad front. By the morning of July 9, they captured the Daugavpils-Vilnius railway ahead of the date scheduled by General Headquarters. The following day, the army's advance units straddled the Daugavpils-Kaunas road.

By that time, the main forces of the 39th Army had managed to reach the front line, and on the morning of July 10 started to advance on Ukmerge.

Delighted with the success of the 43rd and 39th armies, we looked back with apprehension at the powerful Daugavpils grouping of the enemy which had tied down our 6th Guards Army, making the front's right wing lag behind increasingly. Therefore, as soon as Beloborodov reported that his formations had reached the Daugavpils-Kaunas road, we decided to employ some of the 43rd Army's forces to help deal with the Daugavpils grouping.

The troops of the First Baltic Front repelled the enemy's growing number of counterattacks, and by the end of July 15, advanced up to 4 to 8 miles on the northern wing and up to 12 to 20 miles in the center and on the southern wing.

The anxiously awaited 2nd Guards and the 51st armies which the front received from the reserve of General Headquarters were then approaching the front line. The commanders of these armies, their generals and officers, had already arrived at the front command post.

Now, directing the front's main forces toward Kaunas was a pointless and risky affair. Marshal Vasilevsky, who visited us and considered all the pros and cons, ordered the main blow to be directed toward Šiualiai.

On July 18, I ordered Commander of the 51st Army Lieutenant-General Kreyzer to replace the troops of the 43rd Army with advanced formations on the night of July 20 and Commander of the 2nd Guards Army, Lieutenant-General Chanchibadze, to deploy his divisions to the left of the 51st Army. In this way the army commanders would ensure the deployment of their armies' main forces before the offensive on the morning of July 21.

The 51st Army was to deliver the main blow by its left flank and to take Panevežys by July 24; it was to push the offensive toward Šiauliai. The right flank of the 2nd Guards Army was to move in the general direction of Ramigala and Citovjani.

The 3rd Guards Mechanized Corps, which we received from the Third Byelorussian Front, needed replacements in men and materiel, so we decided to let it take part in the fighting after we had seized the Panevežys area, for a strike at Šiauliai.

Meanwhile, the other armies of the front were also setting up their own strike forces. In concentrating their main forces along major directions, the commanders deliberately ran a certain risk.

The 51st and 2nd Guards armies proceeded toward a determined offensive after a short but intensive artillery preparation. The first report from the 2nd Guards and 51st armies said the enemy was showing fierce resistance. But the news improved by midday, when our troops started liberating one town or village after another. By the evening they amounted to dozens.

The front command was somewhat disconcerted by the slow progress of the troops of the 6th Guards and 43rd armies in the Daugavpil area and northwest of the city compared with the success of the newly arrived armies. But let me say in advance that the persistent attacks of the 6th Guards Army did play a positive role. By fighting in the southern suburb of Daugavpils, they tied down most of the enemy's defending forces and assisted the 4th Army, which had surrounded the city from the north from July 24.

On July 27, the 4th Strike Army, acting in conjunction with General Chistyakov's guardsmen, defeated the Daugavpils garrison once and for all. Now I could order the commanders of the 51st and 2nd Guards armies to step up their offensive and reach the line between the towns of Šiauliai and Raseiniai.

To help the 51st Army capture Šiauliai, the 3rd Guards Mechanized Corps took part in the fighting in the morning of July 26, while General Kreyzer brought into action his second wave, the 1st Guards Corps.

The fresh formations advanced quickly and covered 22 to 45 miles in one day. On reaching the River Muša, they disconnected the railway between Šiauliai and Biržai. By the evening of the same day, we received a message from General Obukhov that the advance units of the 3rd Guards Mechanized Corps had engaged the enemy in the southwest suburb of Šiualiai. We were all overjoyed at such marvelous success.

Not wishing to involve armored and motorized units in house-to-house fighting, I ordered the commanders of the infantry formations to step up their troops' advance. Army Commander Kreyzer showed great persistence, and the next day his army, in conjunction with the units of General Obukhov's motorized corps, stormed the key center of the Germans' resistance in the Baltic area.

The 2nd Guards Army also did well, its right-flank divisions having advanced 12 to 25 miles.

During our troops' rapid offensive toward Šiauliai, the chief of staff and I scanned apprehensively the vast map on which the officers of the operations department had drawn in a broken red line the 250-mile salient of our front. The salient which our armies had formed was gradually becoming a thin thread. We had no major reserves left, a situation which could have grave consequences.

Further advance of the armies westward when the other Baltic fronts could not catch up with us, while the Germans continued to show the same resistance in Estonia and Latvia, could be both dangerous and senseless.

We shared our apprehensions with the representative of the Supreme Command. Without hesitation he ordered the 3rd Mechanized Corps and the 51st Army to turn toward Riga, promising the Supreme Command's consent to this move. The capture of Šiauliai made it necessary to turn the front's main forces against the Riga enemy grouping, strike a blow against it, and thus help the troops of the Second and Third Baltic fronts encircle and capture the city.

The same evening, the front armies received their orders: the commander of the 51st Army was immediately to send his troops after the motorized corps which was successfully advancing along the Šiauliai-Jelgava road; the commander of the 2nd Guards Army was to receive from the 51st Army a sector of the front line in the Šiauliai area and to continue the offensive westward on a broad front. The 6th Guards and the 43rd armies were to force the enemy to the right bank of the Daugava.

By the end of the day we received good news from the commander of the 3rd Guards Mechanized Corps. General Obukhov reported: "An advance unit covered 38 miles in one day, approached Jelgava, and engaged the units of the 281st Division of home troops which had come up from Riga."

That was not a bad beginning, since the Gulf of Riga was only 22–25 miles away. I immediately gave orders for part of the corps to move to the gulf and General Kreyzer's infantry formations, which were not so mobile, to come to the mechanized corps's assistance as soon as possible.

General Obukhov wasted no time. While his main forces were fighting for Jelgava, he moved the 8th Guards Mechanized Brigade commanded by the courageous Colonel Kremer toward the Gulf of Riga. The brigade made a 38-mile dash, and stormed and captured the town of Tukums; the brigade's advance unit moved farther north and reached the shore of the Gulf of Riga in the Klapkalns area.

This development was of enormous advantage to us. We had intercepted, though with rather inconsiderable forces, the last land communication between Army Group North and the rest of the German forces. The arrival of our units at the shore of the Gulf of Riga was reported immediately to Moscow.

Realizing that it was difficult to conduct street fighting

in Jelgava with a mechanized corps, I ordered the commander of the 51st Army to perform this task. Knowing General Kreyzer as a past master of surprise attacks who always acted boldly and daringly, I was sure that he would also make short work of the Jelgava enemy grouping. I was right. On receiving his orders, General Kreyzer went personally to the Jelgava area and organized the storming of the besieged town skillfully. The enemy garrison was routed, and by early August the Nazis had lost control of Jelgava.

Marshall Vasilevsky, the representative of the Supreme Command, who was then coordinating the operations of the three Baltic fronts, was concerned that the Nazi troops might slip into East Prussia. He therefore urged our front-line staff to do everything to uncover the real intentions of the German military command, to find out where the enemy was preparing to strike his main blow in order to relieve his grouping in the Baltic region. There was no doubt that an attempt of this kind would be made. But where? The front stretched for 150 miles: from the Riga Gulf shore to Kedainiai.

We learned from a report by General Chanchibadze, commander of the 2nd Guards Army, that his left flank had been attacked on July 28 northwest of Kedainiai by two strong groups of tanks and motorized infantry (6 to 8 motorized regiments and up to 150 tanks). They struck at a gap formed between the 11th and 13th Guards Corps. Later events showed that this was the first in a series of counterblows intended by the German Command for the purpose of helping its troops which had been cut off.

The attack by enemy tanks at the rear of the 32nd Guards Rifle Division forced it to retreat to the northwest. The position at the left flank of the 2nd Guards Army deteriorated sharply. A fierce engagement followed. Both sides fought equally stubbornly, each attack followed by a counterattack. General Chanchibadze rallied his main forces promptly and inflicted heavy losses on the enemy, which made him stop his attacks for the time being.

The first enemy onslaught came up against the Soviet Guards' determination. I had to send my reserve, the 1st Tank Corps, to the army to stabilize the situation in the area.

Then came alarming news from the 43rd Army. In one day its troops had liberated 50 villages and hamlets, repulsing over 15 counterattacks during their offensive. This meant intensive activity on the part of the enemy group concentrated in the Riga area.

An analysis of all the data received by my staff indicated that all the events which had taken place were linked closely. There was no doubt that the enemy was preparing powerful counterblows from different directions against our main forces which had reached the main land communications of Army Group North. We would have to repel these blows to hold our ground whatever the cost.

For this reason, the commander of the 43rd Army was immediately given the order to speed up the march to the River Memele, to consolidate the area, and prepare to repulse a counterblow expected from the north.

But as soon as we began taking these precautionary measures, the commander of the 43rd Army reported that the enemy had struck a powerful counterblow in the general direction of Biržai.

Thanks to measures which were taken immediately, the enemy offensive was stopped at the northern outskirts of Biržai by the evening of August 2. But the Germans resumed their attacks on the morning of August 3. Fierce fighting continued throughout the day, and only by evening did the Nazi troops manage to force their way into the town at the cost of enormous losses. There was the threat of an enemy breakthrough to Panevežys in the deep rear of the main grouping of the front-line troops. At this critical hour we brought into action two corps. This marked a turning point. After two days of ruthless fighting, our troops succeeded in smashing the Germans' attack, forcing the survivors across the River Memele, and securing a small bridgehead.

Having reached the River Memele by August, the 43rd Army, in conjunction with the units of the front's right wing, began to prepare a new offensive for the purpose of liberating the entire territory on the left bank of the Daugava.

The German High Command made the most incredible efforts to rescue Army Group North and by the middle of August managed to concentrate a large grouping, including up to seven tank divisions in front of the 51st and 2nd Guards armies, stretching for 150 miles.

On August 16, the 3rd Tank Army delivered two strong blows in the direction of Jelgava and Šiauliai. Suffice it to say that in the direction of Jelgava alone, the Nazis put four Panzer and two infantry divisions against our two infantry divisions. An equally strong force was advancing toward Šiauliai against the 2nd Guards Army. It included three Panzer and two infantry divisions. Both German groupings numbered altogether over 1,000 tanks and assault guns.

The enemy had chosen a highly appropriate time for embarking on a counteroffensive. By that time, the troops of our front had completed two offensive operations without any letup, losing many tanks and self-propelled guns in the process. So the burden of the massive Nazi Panzer attacks was borne by the artillery, including large-caliber weapons.

On August 21, the Germans launched a combined blow from different directions at the troops of the 51st Army in the Tukums area, where one of the divisions of the 1st Guards Infantry Corps held a front more than 30 miles long. The enemy landed a sizable naval force on the shore of the Gulf of Riga to assist its strike grouping.

With such overwhelming superiority, the enemy managed to capture the road from Tukums to Riga. That was our only major setback throughout the fighting in the Baltic region.

August 26 was a turning point. As guard units began to be brought in at the most dangerous section of the front, the enemy's pressure began to ease off to a noticeable degree. By the end of the month, the Germans were forced to stop attacking altogether. But for how long?

We expected that after doing the necessary regrouping, the enemy would try to renew its attacks on Jelgava. In any case, the enemy still had enough men and equipment.

The Supreme Command set new objectives for the Soviet troops, the aim being to put an end to Army Group North once and for all.

The Leningrad Front was to strike the main blow from the Tartu area, eliminate the enemy's Narva grouping, and then advance toward Tallinn.

The troops of the Third Baltic Front, delivering the main blow with its front flank, were to advance on Riga from the northeast.

The Second Baltic Front, in cooperation with the Third and First Baltic fronts, were to eliminate the enemy troops, maintaining a defensive position north of the Daugava and capture Riga.

The First Baltic Front, employing the troops of the 51st, 6th Guards, and 2nd Guards armies, was ordered to hold its positions at all costs, exhaust the enemy Panzer units in defensive fighting, and prevent their breaking through to Jelgava and Šiauliai. At the same time, the Večmuja and Jecava areas were to be captured at the front's right wing with the troops of the 4th Shock and the 43rd armies, assisted by the 3rd Guard Motorized Corps. They were then to advance farther to the mouth of the Daugava River and make it impossible for the Nazi troops to retreat to Kurland.

The operation was to start on September 5–7. It was a strategic operation extending 300 miles and involving 12 armies—nearly three-quarters of the four fronts.

Unfortunately, we had very little time to prepare the offensive—a week at the most. An enormous amount of work had to be done in that time: reconnoiter the enemy defenses, perform secret regroupings, stock up on shells and other ammunition, and carry out many other measures essential for the success of the planned offensive.

Our greatest difficulty was in preparing to make a forced crossing of the deep and swampy rivers Memele and Lielupe. We were short of standard crossing equipment, while the preparation of improvised equipment required time. Then General Kosyrev, who was in charge of the front engineering service, had the idea of erecting a temporary dam in the upper reaches of the Memele, which would make the river more shallow and create a large number of fords. Bridges from prefabricated materiels were to be put up later across the Lielupe for motor vehicles.

Stalin, the Supreme Commander-in-Chief who was closely following the preparation for the operation, decided that we had not done everything necessary and gave permission for the offensive to be postponed until September 15. We were granted another week, which was very welcome. The week enabled us to devote more time to linking up all the different aspects of the complex front mechanism and see to all the minor details which could have bearing on the way the future operation evolved.

The headquarters of the front and the headquarters of the 43rd and the 4th Strike armies were putting the final touches to the plans for the offensive; they coordinated cooperation between the army troops and the air force and specified at what points the enemy defenses were to be broken through.

Two days before the operation, Generals Malyshev and Beloborodov reported that their armies were ready for action. We reported to Marshal Vasilevsky, and he gave permission for the operation to be brought forward to September 14. The commanding general of the front engineering troops received orders to close the dam. The water level in the river which Beloborodov's and Malyshev's troops were to cross began to drop noticeably. At dawn we went to the command post of the General Beloborodov, who was already there. He did not like the weather, and with good reason. After the rain, everything was shrouded in a thick autumn fog. There was no question of using aircraft because the artillery could fire only blindly.

We decided to begin the attack at a later hour. The fog took a long time to clear, and the waiting was intolerable. By noon, however, the weather improved enough for the army commander to order to begin the artillery and aircraft preparation. The customary booming of the guns began while the planes roared overhead. They flew on several levels: fighters on top, bombers somewhat lower, and screeching attack planes which literally razed the ground.

At 1:00 P.M. the troops of the 43rd and 4th Strike armies successfully attacked the enemy positions. The first results soon became known. Strike army groups crossed the River Memele without much difficulty, breached the enemy defense at an 18-mile stretch, and continued to move north. The enemy showed fierce resistance. The Germans mounted 17 counterattacks in just the second half of the day. But still we broke through his second-defense echelon before dark.

In order to develop our success, we decided to bring the 3rd Guard Mechanized Corps into the breach. General Obukhov brought his advance units toward the town of Ječava, before which ran the enemy's third defense line.

It was already dark, and the advance Soviet units ran into organized resistance and had to stop. The next morning, the defense area became the scene of stubborn fighting. Advance units of the rifle divisions quickly came to the help of the mechanized corps units.

Information obtained during the battle convinced me that it would be senseless to engage in heavy fighting at the approaches to Ječava, where the enemy had powerful defenses. This would only play into the hands of the enemy, who needed time to redeploy his reserves. So I ordered Obukhov's mechanized corps to go around Ječava from the east and to push the offensive toward the Daugava and Riga. General Obukhov carried out the maneuver with great skill. Having left the rifle units near Ječava, he circled the town with his tank and motorized brigades and began quickly to move forward, pushing back the reserves brought in by the enemy from the rear. He was followed by the divisions of the 1st Rifle Corps.

It was the third day of the offensive. Our troops were advancing successfully toward Riga. In the evening General Beloborodov reported that the advance units of the 3rd Guards Mechanized Corps and of the rifle corps of the 43rd Army had fought their way through to the town of Baldone and reached the Daugava.

I looked at the map: a mere 12 miles to Riga. It was easy to see that the appearance of the troops of the front on the southwestern approaches to Riga definitely threatened the isolation and disintegration of entire Army Group North. We also realized that the German command would certainly deliver strong counterblows to repulse the onslaught of the 4th Strike and 43rd armies, which threatened Riga from the southeast. The enemy would take such a course of action if only to escape the net we had laid in wait for him. Our suspicions were soon confirmed.

It was later confirmed that on September 15 General Schoerner, Commander of Army Group North, urged Hitler persistently to allow the withdrawal of his troops from the Soviet Baltic region lest they be totally wiped out. The abnormally stubborn Fuehrer was forced this time to yield and permit the withdrawal of armies defending the front from the Gulf of Finland to the Daugava.

While General Schoerner was gathering up strength on the southern approaches to Riga, his troops in the Dobele area mounted a new and powerful counterblow on September 17, in which over 12 motorized battalions and 380 tanks and assault guns participated. The entire grouping launched an attack against the 51st Army.

The front command was faced with the tasks of guiding the continuing advance toward Riga and repulsing the counterblow.

On the day when the troops of the 3rd German Panzer Army resumed the offensive in the Dobele area, Generals Beloborodov and Malyshev reported new successes in the direction of Riga: a large number of large villages and towns had been liberated as the units of the 43rd and 4th Strike armies launched fierce attacks. At the same time, the army commanders noted that the Nazi troops were showing more resistance as they threw new reserves into counterattacks. Whereas on September 16 our troops advanced 6 to 10 miles, on September 17 the offensive advanced a mere 1 to 2 miles. Our troops encountered more and more enemy units which previously had fought at adjacent sectors of the front.

On the morning of September 19, an enemy strike grouping comprising six divisions, two of them Panzers, and supported from the air, dealt a strong counterblow at the 43rd Army and the units of the 3rd Guards Mechanized Corps. But it was repulsed with heavy losses for the enemy. Our troops continued to advance steadily.

The fighting reached a climax in the last ten days of September. While in the Dobele area, the enemy pushed our troops back 3 miles at an enormous cost in manpower, and he was forced to withdraw toward Riga and to leave Baldone on September 22. All attempts by the Germans to regain Baldone came to nothing despite the arrival of two infantry divisions from Estonia.

Heavy fighting by the Soviet troops during the month of September on the approaches to Riga tied down considerable forces of Army Group North, compelled them to use up nearly all of their reserves, and made it easy for the troops of the Second and Third Baltic fronts to launch an offensive.

In view of the dramatic change in the strategic situation in the Baltic, GHQ found it unnecessary for the troops of the First Baltic Front to launch a further offensive on Riga. The resulting situation required that the troops direct most of their efforts from Riga to Klaipeda, to break through to the sea by a strong, sharp blow westward from the Šiauliai area and to cut through Army Group North's path of retreat to East Prussia. GHQ gave this mission to the troops of the First Baltic Front, and it was accomplished by the middle of October 1944.

12. The Storming of Königsberg

Chief Marshal of the Air Force Alexander Novikov (1900–1976) served in the armed forces from 1919 until 1956, commanded the air force of the Leningrad Front during the first period of the war with Germany, and was Commander of the Soviet Army's Air Force from May 1943 until the end of the war. After the war, he was Commander of Long-Range Military Aviation and Deputy Commander-in-Chief of the Soviet Army Air Force. He retired in 1956 for health reasons and became head of the Higher Civil Aviation School, where he held the title of professor.

During the events described below, he was Commander of the Soviet Army Air Force and Deputy Minister of Defense of the Soviet Union.

O n the night of February 23, 1945, the Kremlin phone jangled on my table. I picked up the receiver and heard Stalin's unhurried, muffled voice. He greeted me and said without any preliminaries, "Can you go and see Vasilevsky?"

"When do you want me to, Comrade Stalin?"

"The sooner the better. Vasilevsky has just phoned me and made an urgent request that I send for you."

Before leaving for the front, I studied the situation in East Prussia. At that time our troops, having cut Army Group Center into three parts during the January offensive, were fighting to eliminate the enemy grouping which was on the defensive south of Königsberg. This grouping of about 20 divisions which relied on a system of permanent fortifications and advantageous positions put up a fierce and stubborn resistance.

At the Rastenburg airfield, we were greeted by Colonel-General Khryukin, Commander of the 1st Air Army. At his HQ I was made familiar with the situation in the 1st Air Army and then went to see Vasilevsky. He outlined the plan of the operation: first the Soviet groups were to rout the Heilsberg grouping, then take Königsberg by storm and finish the operation by wiping out the Samland grouping. The operation began on March 13. The grouping was broken up with the support of the 1st and 3rd Air Armies and was totally eliminated on March 29.

Then it was the turn of Königsberg. The Soviet Command clearly realized what a formidable stronghold Königsberg was. Its big garrison was very well armed and protected from both land and air attacks. The city's defenses were manned by nearly 130,000 officers and men, supported by up to 4,000 guns and mortars and over 100 tanks and assault guns. Based in the airfields of the Samland peninsula—in Gross Dirschkeim, Gross Hubniken, and Neutife—were 170 warplanes. The Germans had built four lines of defense around and inside the city. The ancient castle in the center was manned by several thousand troops. From the air Königsberg was protected by 56 AA batteries (nearly 450 guns). The city had underground factories and sufficient supplies of materiel and rations.

The Soviet Command entrusted General Bagramyan with the task of capturing the city and eliminating the Samland grouping, and he and his assistants coped with the difficult assignment quickly and efficiently.

The command ordered four field armies to defeat the

Königsberg grouping. The 43rd and 50th armies were to attack from the north, the 11th Guards Army from the south, and the 39th Army was to cut off the fortress for the Samland enemy grouping.

Air support was provided by the 1st, 3rd, and 18th Air armies, the Air Force of the Baltic Fleet, and the 5th Guards and 5th Bomber Corps. On the day the storming was to take place the front had a total of 2,444 combat aircraft, including 1,124 bombers, 470 attack planes, 830 fighters, and 20 torpedo aircraft.

We realized that although aircraft was to play a great role in capturing the city, the last word was still with the infantry, and the main objective of the air force was to give it every possible assistance. We therefore did everything to give the front not only a powerful bomber group, but also a strong attack aircraft group which included six attack plane divisions.

We paid particular attention to the plan of using the attack planes in the Königsberg operation for combat purposes, making sure that the attack planes were striking where it was most effective—i.e., that the strikes were dealt simultaneously and continuously on the whole of the enemy's tactical defense. To this end, the strikes of attack-plane formations were made in two waves. The first one (up to two-thirds of the forces) directly supported the troops in the battlefield, striking at the enemy defense to a depth of 1 mile, while the second attacked the enemy at a distance of 2 or more miles from the front line, neutralized artillery, and prevented the retreating Germans from taking up intermediate positions and their reserves from reaching the area of combat operations.

The plan provided for carrying out a preliminary air preparation for two days before the city was to be stormed. The objective was to destroy the forts and key strongpoints in the zones of advance of the 43rd and 11th Guards armies, mount massive raids on the enemy air force on the ground, and destroy their runways. Strikes by attack-plane formations were to complete the destruction of the enemy air force. Another objective was an additional thorough air reconnaissance of the combat areas.

On the first day of the operation, before the general attack, 406 bombers and 133 bomb-carrying fighters would launch a massive strike against the enemy positions before the front of the advancing armies. Then the attack planes would go into action, accompanying the infantry and tanks and wiping out the enemy's fire emplacements which had been restored or had been previously undetected.

High-aviation density (240 combat planes per mile of the front in main sectors) required a high degree of precision in take-off and return schedules. Demarcation flight lines were established for every formation; all air divisions had their own routes and flight altitudes to the target and back. Low-altitude group flights over airfields were strictly forbidden. Bonfires were to be lit along the front line to help pilots flying at night find their bearings, while Königsberg's center was to be marked by a crisscross of searchlights.

Special emphasis was given to the details concerning the cooperation between the air force and the ground troops. To this end, large mockups of the enemy defensive lines were constructed on which all the commanders of air units had training sessions. Three days before the operation, the commanders of air corps and divisions were issued with photo maps of the city, charts, maps with numbered targets, and instructions on the combat use of aircraft.

On the eve of the storming operation, officers who specialized in electronic guidance of aircraft on targets joined the breakthrough units, and air force representatives who were in charge of controlling the attack plane units directly cooperating with the attacking troops arrived at the command posts of field armies.

At last the operation was ready to be carried out. On or about April 3, Marshal Vasilevsky phoned Moscow in my presence and reported the front's readiness to storm

Königsberg. After hearing a brief report, Stalin said that the enemy should be wiped out as soon as possible in East Prussia.

"The Commander-in-Chief is in a hurry," Vasilevsky said as he replaced the receiver. "There is little time left till the Berlin operation."

Bad weather was interfering with the preliminary air preparation. Nevertheless, we hoped to make our preparations even if only partially. But April 4 also brought bad news for the airmen. Before dawn a dense fog covered the ground. It remained for a long time; then the rain began and grew heavier. There was a thick gray mist everywhere, and even large objects could be seen only in outline.

At night the weather somewhat improved and I ordered two divisions of Po-2 light night bombers to be sent up. These were not actually combat planes, but training planes adapted to fly over the front line in close formation, and designed to strike at individual targets. They flew only at night because they were quite defenseless against fighters and could not be used against strongpoints. A Po-2 carried only 440 lb. of bombs: two bombs of 220 lb. or four of 110 lb. No more was necessary where manpower or smaller objects were concerned.

The Germans detested these lightweight planes made from wood and cotton percale which night after night hung over the enemy positions and harassed the Nazis by frequent and unexpected raids. As a rule, Po-2s dropped their bombs at night, with the engines cut off, flying over the enemy so suddenly and at such low altitudes that they were virtually invulnerable.

On the night of April 4, the Po-2s performed 657 missions. Twin-engine bombers flew just over 100 sorties. An attempt to use the heavy machines of the 18th Air Army was not successful. Of the 40 heavy bombers that took off, only 15 reached the city and dropped their bombs; the rest lost their bearings and returned to base without fulfilling their mission.

Bad weather interrupted our plan for air preparation. Our artillerymen had no better luck either. Poor visibility prevented them from opening up the enemy's forts and pillboxes by blasting off the protective layers of earth.

We spent a whole day impatiently, waiting for flying weather. On the morning of April 6, I arrived at the command post of the 43rd Army Commander, General Beloborodov. It was located in an old house on a gentle slope in the Fuchsberg area northwest of Königsberg. Marshal Vasilevsky and General of the Army Bagramyan, Commander of the First Baltic Front, soon arrived there, too.

The last minutes before the storming were especially frustrating. Then, at about 9:00 A.M., the guns of the 11th Guards Army began to boom somewhere south of Königsberg. An hour later, the artillery of other armies also opened fire.

The pounding of the enemy defenses lasted for more than two hours. The ground literally shuddered from the salvos of superpowerful guns. Rockets screeched as they left behind fiery trails. "The God of War," as we called artillery, performed its part with precision, skill, and a good display of strength. Our artillerymen were doing a superb job, and Vasilevsky found a moment to put down his binoculars and say, "That's quite a concert!"

At 12:00 P.M. sharp it suddenly fell quiet and then storming columns and assault tanks rushed forward to attack. Then something happened that could only have been expected. The command post was fired at suddenly by at least a battalion of enemy artillery. Several shells hit a group of military lawyers who had come to the command post to see the commencement of the storming operation. They had been warned that to let themselves be seen by the enemy as they did was extremely dangerous, but they ignored this warning and paid dearly for their mistake. Several were killed outright; others were wounded.

The shells exploded next to the house. The windowpane in the room where Bagramyan and Beloborodov were was shattered by the blast wave. Beloborodov was hurled into a corner, and Bagramyan's face was cut with glass splinters.

This was clearly no accident. After Königsberg had been taken, one of the Nazi generals taken prisoner admitted during interrogation they had some time previously noticed the big house on the hill and watched it in expectation for a suitable opportunity to shell it.

By that time the weather had improved somewhat, and I ordered that aircraft be sent to accompany the infantry—attack planes and fighters trained for action over battlefield. But they were to join the battle in small groups. The smoke and dust raised by shell explosions were too dense for proper orientation, and the smallest act of carelessness could result in our own troops being hit.

By 2:00 P.M. the airmen had flown only about 300 missions. Then bombers joined the action one by one. They struck mainly at the northwestern outskirts of the city and the railway junction. During the day, the bombers made only 85 sorties instead of the planned 1,218.

Enemy planes offered almost no resistance. During the day, there were only two dogfights, which were brief and not intentional. Though we were masters of the situation in the air, we failed to take full advantage of our superiority. Bad weather grounded most of the bombardment and assault aircraft, while the naval aviation could not operate because of the heavy fog.

Lack of strong pressure on the enemy from the air had a marked effect on the ground troops. By the close of the day, the infantry had advanced only 1 to 2 miles. The main strongpoints and centers of enemy defense could not be neutralized despite a prolonged artillery preparation. The infantry and tanks which had wedged into the enemy's battle formations hindered the massive employment of our artillery. In such a situation, fighting threatened to become protracted. In addition, the German High Command, having felt the impact of the blows of our 39th Army whose units had cut off the Königsberg-Pillau railway, quickly transferred infantry and antitank units and part of the 5th Panzer Division from the Samland peninsula to the combat area.

As soon as the fog had cleared, our attack planes hung over the enemy positions. The planes of the 11th Fighter Corps delivered several strikes at the airfields in Gross Dirschkeim and Gross Hubniken, which were later fully blocked from the air.

From 10:00 A.M. on the bombers of the 1st and 3rd Air armies and the 5th Guards Bomber Corps joined battle. As many as 246 bombers delivered three powerful strikes in succession at the areas where the enemy's resistance was strongest, mostly at the troops fighting west of Königsberg. Soviet infantry and tanks, constantly accompanied by attack planes, crossed the enemy's third line of defense at many points and broke through into the city during the second half of the day. House-to-house fighting began.

In any battle, the moment comes sooner or later when one strong extra blow can finally tip the scale in one's favor. A simple truth, but the trick is to take advantage of the moment when it appears.

The first signs of a favorable opportunity began to appear after noon. At about that time, I contacted Vasilevsky and asked if it wasn't the time to bring into action the main strike force of our aviation, the 18th Air Army. The weather was good, and the airmen could bomb individual targets instead of resorting to blanket bombing. The marshal thought for a moment and agreed. I immediately gave the necessary orders.

While the heavy machines were flying to Königsberg, we carried out another preventive measure twenty minutes before they appeared over the city: 118 aircraft attacked and bombed the enemy airfields where fighters were based.

The first planes of the 18th Air Army had now appeared. They followed one another at equal intervals. The noise of the bombing continued over Königsberg for nearly an hour. A total of 3,743 bombs weighing 550 tons altogether were dropped. The entire city was shrouded in smoke. The massive strike by 516 planes had had its effect. Many strongpoints and forts had been demolished, traffic in the city stopped, and the garrison command, as was later borne out during prisoner interrogation, lost control of its units and could not maneuver its reserves. The enemy's resistance dropped sharply as a result, and other troops began to move more quickly to the center of Königsberg.

During the second half of the day, air reconnaissance reported that the enemy was bringing in fresh troops from the Samland peninsula in order to prevent our encirclement of Königsberg. Attack planes were ordered to disrupt the enemy plan. Up until twilight, they attacked Nazi troops concentrated in the forests west of the city and frustrated the enemy's attempt to deliver a counterblow.

The same day, the Germans tried to rectify the situation by interfering with the operations of our air force, but Soviet airmen put a quick and decisive end to these attempts. Sixteen enemy planes were shot down in 22 dogfights, and 36 were destroyed on the airfields. We lost 25 planes.

On April 7, our airmen had to work hard: they made over 4,700 sorties and dropped over 1,600 tons of bombs. That was not the limit, however, and for April 8 we planned over 6,000 missions.

On April 8, the Soviet Air Force made all-out efforts. The airmen's combat work continued until dark. Heavy night bombers attacked the port of Pillau and the road junction at Fischhausen through which most of the enemy's troops passed. At dawn, attack planes and day bombers took off. Some of them bombed the enemy in Königsberg itself while others bombed the infantry and tanks west of

the city. Our infantry and tanks, covered constantly by
attack planes, cut short enemy counterattacks and advanced to the city center. During the second half of the
day, the troops of the 43rd Army drove the Germans out of
the entire northwestern area of Königsberg, while the troops
of the 11th Guards Army made a forced crossing of the
River Pregel. The advanced units of these armies soon
linked up at Amalienau and thus closed the ring around the
city.

Our attack planes were a great help to the ground troops.
The first to reach the River Pregel was the 16th Guards
Rifle Division commanded by General Pronin; but because
of the strong enemy fire, the division's troops could not
make a forced crossing from march column. Then the air
force representative in the division called in attack planes.
Three six-plane groups first put an end to the enemy
artillery, then held down the Nazi infantry by bomb-and-
gun fire. Covered by attack planes, the Soviet infantry
crossed the river quickly.

The noose around the remnants of the Königsberg garrison was getting tighter. The Germans held on to the bitter
end at the citadel and other fortifications in the city center
and were making ready to launch a strike from the outside
to lead the troops out of the fortress. General Müller, who
was commanding the 4th German Army, once again began
to concentrate forces west of Königsberg in order to make
a strike which would relieve the enemy troops and ordered
the fortress commander to deliver a strike from the other
direction.

The air force was called in to foil this plan. We employed the main forces of the 3rd and 18th Air armies
against the enemy troops concentrated west of the city.
Bombers' strikes were followed by strikes by attack planes
and fighters. The sound of exploding bombs went on all
day and all night west of Königsberg.

The fate of those still remaining in the Königsberg
garrison was sealed. The final stage of the storming opera-

tion began on the morning of April 9, when several thousand guns and mortars opened devastating fire on the fortress and the last strongpoints of German defense. The air force had little to do in the city itself, so small groups of planes struck at the racecourse and airport in order to prevent German transport planes from landing and flying out the garrison's top command.

The main task of the Soviet air force that day was to wipe out the enemy troops west of Königsberg. Almost all aircraft operating on April 9 were redirected toward that area.

By the end of the day, the enemy lay down arms. An impregnable fortress that had a strong and well-armed garrison concealed between the exceptionally thick walls of the ancient forts and pillboxes and immense supplies of materiel and foodstuffs—everything required for long resistance—was destroyed in just four days. This was a truly brilliant victory of the Soviet Army, and yet more proof of its might, operational and tactical skill, and the heroism of its soldiers.

13. The Capture of Budapest

Marshal of the Soviet Union Matvei Zakharov (1898–1972) began army service in 1917. When the Second World War broke out, he was an Army Chief of Staff and later Chief of Staff of a number of fronts. After the war, he was Commander of the Military Academy of the General Staff, commander of a military district, Commander-in-Chief of the Group of Soviet Forces in Germany, and later Chief of the General Staff of the Soviet Army.

In late September 1944 the troops of the Second Ukrainian Front, of which I was chief of staff, began to carry out operations for the liberation of Hungary. By that time Romania had been completely liberated, and one-third of Hungarian territory with one-fourth of the country's population had been cleared of Nazi occupying forces.

The entry of Soviet troops into Hungary provided a fresh impetus for the struggle of the people against the fascist occupation regime. People's self-government bodies began to emerge in the liberated territory, and the question arose of forming a new democratic government which would break away from Nazi Germany and declare war on it.

In view of the weak position of the ruling clique in Szalasist Hungary, the General Headquarters of the Soviet Supreme Command instructed Marshal of the Soviet Union Malinovsky, Commander of the Second Ukrainian Front, to mount a new offensive on October 29, 1944, with the ultimate aim of liberating the Hungarian capital and securing Hungary's withdrawal from the war. The main blow was to be delivered by the left flank of the Second Ukrainian Front in an area between the Tisza and the Danube, which was defended chiefly by the troops of the hastily formed 3rd Hungarian Army.

Commander of the 46th Army General Shlemin displayed great energy. Launching an offensive on October 29, his troops broke through enemy defenses later on the same day, while the 2nd and 4th Mechanized Corps brought into the breach reached the outer defenses of the Hungarian capital by November 2. However, the attempt of our troops to burst into the capital and engage the enemy in street fighting failed.

Alarmed by the possible loss of Budapest, the German Command rapidly transferred large forces to an area between the Tisza and the Danube and, with their defense lines built earlier, the Germans were able to halt the Soviet offensive temporarily.

By November 4 the right flank of our troops advancing on Budapest began to be threatened by an armored thrust. Under these circumstances, GHQ issued orders that the attack on the Hungarian capital be stopped and the armies be brought to the western bank of the Tisza, where they were to mount a large-scale offensive with the aim of defeating the Budapest enemy grouping by attacking it from the north and northeast in cooperation with the left wing of the front attacking from the south.

On November 11, 1944, the Soviet troops of the center and right wing of the Second Ukrainian Front launched an offensive and in 16 days of heavy fighting destroyed considerable enemy forces and liberated many Hungarian towns and villages. But the main task of destroying the Budapest grouping was not achieved.

Nor was it achieved during the third assault on Budapest, mounted on the night of December 5, 1944, when the troops of the 46th Army forced a crossing of the Danube south of Budapest.

Having secured a bridgehead on the right bank of the river, the army nevertheless failed to break through strong enemy defenses from march column. This was due to the fatigue of the troops, which had been on the offensive for several months, the mud season, and nonflying weather.

Having considerably reinforced his position by moving tanks toward Budapest, the enemy put up fierce resistance. Having lost hope of holding on to Germany's central and northern regions, the Nazi clique decided to escape to its southern part and Austria behind a large mountain range. There they intended to remain until a clash occurred between the Soviet and Anglo-American forces in Europe, which they believed to be inevitable. The Nazis spared no efforts and resources to hold Hungary and built several defense lines within a relatively short time. The strongest one ran along the right bank of the Danube and included the fortified area of Budapest. It consisted of three well-organized horseshoe-shaped positions extending to the Danube north and south of the Hungarian capital.

That was why fierce fighting raged during the Budapest operation and it was so difficult for the troops of one front to destroy the enemy grouping. But despite the difficulties, after a 45-day offensive, the troops of the Second Ukrainian Front reached the Danube north of Budapest and the Czechoslovak border on the River Ipel. The right wing of the front entered Czechoslovak territory.

The active combat operations carried out by the Second Ukrainian Front immobilized a considerable enemy force, thus making it easier for our neighbor on the left—the Third Ukrainian Front—to advance on Hungarian territory lying beyond the Danube. By December 9 its troops reached

Lake Velence, Lake Balaton, and an area south of the River Drawa. Now the task of capturing Budapest could best be achieved by the forces of both fronts.

On December 26, 1944, the two advancing Ukrainian fronts encircled the Budapest enemy grouping and liberated almost the whole of Hungarian territory east of the Danube. The Soviet troops had driven into a pocket 7 infantry, 2 tank, 1 motorized, and 2 cavalry divisions, 3 artillery brigades, about 30 separate regiments and battalions, and various German and Hungarian groups with a total strength of up to 188,000 officers and men.

The most significant political outcome of the Soviet military effort in Hungary in December 1944 was the further consolidation of the country's democratic forces. On December 21, 1944, a Provisional National Assembly met in Debrecen and formed a Provisional National Government from members of the parties of the Hungarian National Independence Front. On December 28 the new government declared war on Hitler's Germany and called upon the Hungarian people to join the new Hungarian armed forces.

The Soviet Command began preparations for the assault on Budapest, doing everything it could to avoid unnecessary bloodshed and the destruction of the ancient city.

On December 29, 1944, at 11:00 A.M., Soviet parliamentaries were sent to the enemy headquarters with an ultimatum signed by the commanders of the Second and Third Ukrainian fronts. Addressing the enemy, Marshal Malinovsky and Marshal Tolbukhin warned that further resistance was useless and could lead only to the destruction of his troops, heavy casualties among the civilian population, and ruin of the Hungarian capital. Those willing to surrender were guaranteed life and unhindered return to their homeland after the war, and the wounded and sick, immediate medical aid. However, Miklos Steinmetz and Ilya Ostapenko, the parliamentaries of the Second and

Third Ukrainian fronts respectively, were killed treacherously by the fascists.

On the first day of the new year, 1945, the Soviet forces mounted an assault on Budapest. The Hitlerites threatened to wipe out the large, ancient city with its historical and cultural monuments and its beautiful bridges over the Danube, dooming its population to suffering and death. The Soviet Command, on the other hand, did its utmost to prevent excessive damage to the city and save its inhabitants.

In the first half of January, the city was attacked by the 18th Separate Guards Rifle Corps, and the 30th Rifle and 7th Romanian army corps. Immediately fierce fighting broke out in Pest. The Germans there had large supplies of materiel and had received ammunition, fuel, and food by air. Occupying buildings situated at street corners, they kept several streets under fire at a time. The fascists felt safe behind the thick walls of old buildings and continued to deliver heavy machine-gun and artillery fire from the windows, apertures, and specially cut gun ports. Many large buildings had been mined in anticipation of the advance of Soviet tanks.

But nothing could halt the Soviet offensive. Overcoming stubborn enemy resistance, the Soviet soldiers cleared one district after another of Nazi troops. On January 9 they seized a racecourse near the eastern railway station which the Germans used as an airfield, thereby stopping their airlifts. Parachute drops were ineffective and often went to the wrong destination.

On January 18 Soviet forces liberated Pest. During their retreat, the Nazis blew up all the bridges over the Danube, the pride of the Hungarian capital. In the fighting in Pest, about 36,000 enemy soldiers were killed. Our forces destroyed and captured 291 tanks and assault guns, 1,419 artillery pieces and mortars, 222 armored vehicles and APCs, 784 machine guns, 20,140 rifles, 2,700 motor vehicles, and a considerable amount of other military equipment.

After the liberation of Pest, the operation to free Buda

got under way. It involved the 18th Separate Guards Rifle Corps of the Second Ukrainian Front, the 7th Romanian Army Corps, and the 37th and 75th Rifle Corps transferred to the Budapest grouping of Soviet troops from the Third Ukrainian Front.

The assault on Buda, situated on the hills, was not an easy one. There every building was turned into a fortress. During the 20 days of offensive operations, our troops managed to seize only 114 out of 722 city blocks. The tenacity of Nazi resistance was also explained by Hitler's promises to get his troops out of the "ring." By the end of January, when the third German attempt to rescue its Budapest grouping failed, the morale of the encircled enemy troops deteriorated drastically. On February 5, after a slight regrouping, the Soviet troops wiped out the strongest pockets of enemy resistance and by the end of February 11 liberated 109 city blocks, capturing 25,000 German officers and men. The operation for eliminating the encircled enemy grouping in Buda lasted 25 days. As in Pest, in an effort to save the architectural monuments in the oldest part of the city, the Soviet Command did not resort to heavy artillery fire or air bombing.

On the night of February 12, 16,000 German officers and men made a last attempt to break out of the trap. They breached the battle formation of our 180th Division, and more than 15,000 enemy officers and men escaped from the city. But they did not go far; by February 14, the entire group was destroyed. A total of 33,000 German officers and men remaining in the city surrendered. On the morning of February 13, 1945, the Hungarian capital was freed from the German occupying force. The defeat of the Budapest grouping opened the way to Austria for the Second and Third Ukrainian fronts. The Soviet headquarters began planning the Vienna offensive.

Having buried the hope of holding the front in eastern Prussia and on the Vistula, the German Command decided to launch active operations in the south in order to deny

Soviet troops access to Austria and southern Germany. They planned to defeat the troops of the Third Ukrainian Front and eliminate the bridgehead on the western bank of the Danube. For this purpose, the 6th SS Panzer Army and the 6th Field Army were to deal the main blow between Lake Balaton and Lake Velence to cut through the Third Ukrainian Front and reach the Danube. Then the main German forces would push the offensive to the north and seize Budapest. Some units were to advance to the south, and, together with the 2nd Panzer Army and the Weichs army group operating in Yugoslavia, destroy the troops of the Third Ukrainian Front south of Lake Balaton.

That the enemy was determined to carry out his plan was evident from the size of the force which was assigned the task of mounting a counteroffensive. It included over 400,000 officers and men, up to 6,000 guns and mortars, 877 tanks and assault guns, 900 armored personnel carriers, and about 850 aircraft. The enemy concentrated over a third of his manpower, nine-tenths of his tanks and assault guns, and more than half of artillery pieces in the main direction of attack. The 6th Panzer Army, made up of crack Nazi troops, had many Tiger and Panther heavy tanks.

Since the Third Ukrainian Front was to bear the brunt of the enemy attack, GHQ did its utmost to reinforce it partly by using reserves but chiefly by transferring considerable forces and materiel from our front. By the time the Third Ukrainian Front assumed the defensive, the Second Ukrainian Front had transferred to it three rifle, two tank, one mechanized, and one cavalry corps, the entire 27th Field Army, as well as a large number of reinforcement units, mainly artillery regiments and brigades.

Needless to say, these measures could not be carried out without affecting the situation on our front, where our troops were already on the offensive on Czechoslovak territory. Therefore, when on February 17 a large enemy grouping including about 400 tanks and assault guns mounted a strong surprise attack from the Komarno region against the 17th Guards Army, it achieved considerable success. Stretched in one echelon over a distance of 75 miles, General Shumilov's army, whose left flank was threatened with encirclement by the evening of February 18, had to abandon the bridgehead on the eastern bank of the Hron River. In order to check the enemy offensive, the commander of the Second Ukrainian Front moved a number of units to that sector of the front.

While the troops of our front were engaged in fierce fighting at the Hron bridgehead, the Third Ukrainian Front had finished preparations to meet the enemy. Waging a defensive operation from March 6 to 15, its troops wore out the enemy and inflicted heavy losses in manpower and materiel. In ten days the Germans lost 40,000 killed, about 500 tanks and assault guns and nearly as many armored personnel carriers, and more than 300 guns and mortars.

Under a directive issued by GHQ on March 9, the Third Ukrainian Front was to be chiefly responsible for the attack in the Vienna operation. As far as we were concerned, when our right wing reached the Hron, we were to take on the rigid defensive in an area north of the Danube. The left wing of the front (46th Army) was to assume the offensive on March 15–16 and, together with the troops of the Third Ukrainian Front, to smash the enemy grouping south of the Danube and push the offensive toward Gyor.

By March 20 the forces of both Ukrainian fronts operating between the Danube and Lake Balaton took part in the Vienna operation. Forced into a pocket south of Lake Balaton, the panic-stricken SS Panzer units retreated hastily, abandoning their arms and other materiel.

From March 16 to March 25, the Nazis suffered a serious defeat in an area between Lake Balaton and the Danube, losing over 50,000 killed and captured, and a considerable quantity of weapons and other military equipment. The troops of both fronts launched pursuit, and on March 31 the 9th Guards Army crossed the Austrian border. On April 4, 1945, the whole of Hungary was liberated from the Nazi occupying forces.

During the capture of Budapest, the troops of the Second Ukrainian Front carried out diverse operations. The offensive began from breaking through the enemy defense lines of different degrees of preparedness. In operational depth, our troops were engaged in fierce fighting, pursued the enemy, and crossed rivers from march column. The offensive was carried out in wide zones, and the combat formations of the units were not deep. Tank and mechanized units advanced in the first wave, together with field armies. This method of employing our tank forces gave excellent results.

When breaking through deliberate defenses on the approaches to Budapest, our rifle units assumed deep battle formations and advanced in narrow zones. In such cases, the density of artillery fire reached over 320 guns and mortars per mile, and the artillery preparation was delivered by fire assaults against enemy strongholds and artillery positions for 40 to 65 minutes. Following a breakthrough of deep enemy defenses, tank, mechanized, and cavalry units were usually sent into the breach to exploit our success. They often had to be employed fully or partly to complete the breakthrough of the tactical zone of defense owing to a lack of tanks to provide direct infantry support. In order to exploit success in the operational depth of defense, units of second echelons were used, along with tank and cavalry units and troops transferred from adjacent sectors of the front.

During the Budapest operation, our troops gained a wealth of experience in capturing a large city.

In this connection, I would like first of all to note the courage and initiative displayed by assault groups, which played a decisive role in the seizure of the Hungarian capital. Supported by fire from large-caliber machine guns, artillery, and tanks, a handful of brave soldiers—submachine gunners, sappers, and flamethrower operators—would unnoticeably approach a building turned by the enemy into a stronghold, throw grenades into its windows, burst into the house, and fight tenaciously for every room and every staircase. At times they had to take along wire cutters, mine detectors, and other devices to breach enemy obstacles.

Normally, assault groups advanced through courtyards and various passageways and gaps rather than along streets in order to take the enemy by surprise. The best time to do so was at night: the Germans feared night fighting.

For humanitarian reasons, the Soviet Command avoided the use of bombers whenever possible. Fighter planes protected the city against enemy bombers and blocked the airlift of weapons, ammunition, and food to encircled troops. Attack planes, in close cooperation with the infantry, delivered blows at hard-to-reach strongholds of enemy resistance, thus facilitating the liberation of the city. I must not omit to mention those who were closest to the earth: the sappers. They were invaluable during the Budapest operation. They secured the crossing of the Tisza and the Danube for our troops and cleared paths through minefields; no assault group could do without them in Budapest. They restored hundreds of miles of highways and gravel roads and dozens of bridges, and dug many miles of trenches.

Our sappers were not only excellent fighters, they also saved the lives of hundreds of thousands of Hungarian civilians. Unlike many cities and towns, where mines were removed after the liberation, the capital of Hungary was cleared of mines while the battles were still going on. To obtain information about mined facilities from the inhabitants of Budapest, special posts were set up where Soviet officers were on round-the-clock duty, together with local interpreters and sapper units. Passing by such posts in those days, one could see long lines of Budapest residents waiting to report on mined facilities. Making use of such reports and displaying skill, resourcefulness, and courage, our sappers checked and cleared 2,450 mined facilities.

If at the beginning of an operation the troops were sometimes controlled from command posts, during a battle the commander of the front and a small team of officers remained with the troops. It was the commander who personally directed the commitment of tank units and second waves to battle, specified the tasks, and assigned new ones in accordance with the changing situation. Assessing the overall picture of battle development and taking into account any changes in the situation, Malinovsky made decisions and took measures which enabled the troops of the front to reach such lines and in such an order as to destroy the enemy in the quickest and most decisive manner.

For more effective control of units, regiment commanders set up their command posts 150 to 300 yards from the forward line. Battalion and company commanders personally organized the seizure of each objective. Superior headquarters often sent their officers to the units to check the latter's actions, eliminate shortcomings on the spot, organize cooperation between units, and see to it that the orders of the commander of a superior unit and the general mission were carried out.

Finally the guns fell silent on Hungarian soil. The fierce bloody battle waged by the Soviet soldiers for the freedom of the Hungarian people ended. Along with the warm spring wind, liberation from the shackles of fascism came to the valley of the Tisza and the Danube.

14. The Fall of Berlin

Marshal of the Soviet Union Vasily Chuikov (1900–1982) was on active service from 1917. At the start of the Second World War, Chuikov was the Soviet military attaché in China. From 1942 onward, he commanded the 62nd Army, subsequently renamed the 8th Guards Army, which battled its way from Stalingrad to Berlin. After the war he was appointed the Supreme Commander of the Soviet forces stationed in Germany. Later he was successively the commander of a military district in the Soviet Union, the Supreme Commander of the Land Forces of the Soviet Union, the Commander of Civil Defense, and a Deputy Minister of Defense of the Soviet Union.

The final assault on Berlin, capital of the Third Reich, began on April 25, 1945.

The troops of the 8th Guards Army under my command assumed assault positions.

On the night before the assault, I inspected the positions of our artillery. I was interested to see how our artillerymen were adjusting their range, and, in general, wanted to impress on my memory the first salvos of our last strike at the Third Reich.

Dark, fluffy clouds were drifting low. A drizzling rain was falling. The earth seemed to slumber, trembling from time to time from distant explosions.

A battery of heavy guns was positioned in a meadow near a forest.

The men and guns were ready for action.

"On the fortifications of Berlin—fire!"

Heavy shells whistled through the air.

From my observation post I could see the full power of the artillery fire that slammed into the enemy positions. House walls with windows turned into firing ports collapsed. Roadblocks and barricades were blown up and flew into the air.

The 8th Guards Army attacked the center of Berlin from the south. The troops formed assault groups that included tanks and artillery pieces of every caliber up to the largest, as well as engineer and mortar units. Those which were to cross water barriers were equipped accordingly. Fighting every inch of the way, they took one city block after another.

The assault continued day and night without letup. That was the whole point of the storming operation. We advanced on Tiergarten along the Landwehr Canal. Our army's zone of advance gradually narrowed to resemble a sharp spear as it drew closer to the center of Berlin. Delivering a concentric blow, all the forces surrounding Berlin and directly participating in the assault (the 2nd Guards Tank, the 3rd and 5th Shock, and the 8th Guards armies of the First Byelorussian Front) had conical sectors of advance. The units of the 1st Guards Army also operated in the 8th Guards Army's zone.

By now we had worked out tactics of employing large tank units in town fighting. Originally, tanks moved along city streets in columns, and this technique was costly. Strung out in a line, the tanks created jams and were easy prey for the Germans' antitank rockets. When the leading tank was set ablaze, the others were trapped, their sides exposed to enemy fire. Therefore, on the very first day of the storming operation, our tankmen reorganized their battle formations. They cooperated closely with the infantry, artillerymen, and engineers. As a result, tank losses were reduced to minimum.

It is much more difficult to fight a battle in a city, especially in one the size of Berlin, than in an open field. The ability of the HQs and commanders of large units to influence the course of combat operations in a city is reduced greatly. Much therefore depends on the initiative of junior commanders and the rank-and-file soldiers. An urban battle in a close-fire combat in which not only automatic weapons, but powerful artillery systems and tank guns, are involved at close quarters, hitting targets only a few dozen yards away. The enemy, hidden in basements and buildings, opens machine-gun fire and hurls grenades as soon as you appear.

An advance through a city takes place in leaps and bounds as troops dash from one captured building to another. But these actions are being carried out on a broad front, on every street. The HQs and their officers operate in close proximity to their particular objectives. It is their job to maintain communications, chiefly by radio, to coordinate the actions of assault groups, organize the collection of intelligence, and see to it that ammunition and rations are supplied in adequate quantities. They also establish a single system of signals for daylight and night hours. The commanders and staff officers organize the closest possible cooperation between all fighting arms in platoons, companies, and battalions, out of which assault groups are formed.

On the first day, our army's assault groups had advanced 2 and on some sectors 2½ miles closer to the city center.

Fighting was fierce in nearly every sector. Every block abounded with fire emplacements and antitank rocket launchers aimed against our tanks and troop concentrations from balconies and top-floor windows.

Berlin's numerous railways crisscrossing the city in every direction formed advantageous defense positions. The approaches to railway stations, bridges, and crossings had been turned into powerful strongpoints and the canals into defense lines at which the enemy attempted to stem our advance. It was no easy matter to operate under these conditions.

The outcome of street fighting depends on the initiative and combat skill of small assault groups. Several soldiers armed with hand grenades, submachine guns, and rifles, and supported by machine guns and mortars will always achieve success if they attack swiftly. The important thing to remember is that you should not move along straight streets, but use holes in walls of buildings, gates, back doors, backyards, and back streets. The enemy usually mines some buildings and the space between them, lays land mines in the streets, and sets up booby traps inside buildings. We taught our soldiers: "Don't move forward until you have reconnoitered the way carefully, and once you are sure of success, attack swiftly and determinedly." The stone buildings which the Germans defended with great stubbornness had to be destroyed by artillery and mortar fire, and their garrisons wiped out with hand grenades.

In order to reach the Tempelhof airfield, we had to cross the Teltow Canal. We learned from prisoners that there were fueled-up planes in underground hangars ready to take off at a moment's notice. Their crews, which were on duty round-the-clock, included pilots and navigators who used to fly Hitler, Goebbels, Bormann, and other leaders of the Third Reich to various parts of Germany. Evidently Hitler and his associates were still in Berlin. We had to prevent them from slipping out through this last escape hatch. The 39th and 79th Guards Rifle divisions were ordered to encircle the airfield, while the artillery was to keep the runways under fire. We had no information about the precise location of the exit from the underground hangars. For this reason, assault groups reinforced with tanks were instructed to cut off the approaches to the runways by machine-gun fire, bottling up the planes underground.

The plan worked beautifully. No plane was allowed to take off from the airfield from the evening of April 25, and by noon on April 26, the entire airport was in our hands.

The storming operation entered its third day. The area still in the hands of the Berlin garrison was shrinking fast, but resistance was stiffening all the time. The density of our battle formations increased, and fire maneuver was reduced to a minimum. Men and equipment were squeezed into the narrow confines of the streets. Now our advance could be compared to the work of miners working a gallery. To advance from one street to another, you drove through gaps in thick brick walls or over heaps of rubble and mountains of broken reinforced concrete and twisted steel. Knowing that the end was near, the Nazis blew up buildings, heedless of the death of civilians.

General Ryzhov, Commander of the 28th Guards Rifle Corps, reported to me that beyond the Heinrich von Kleist Park a besieged enemy garrison occupying a corner building converted into a powerful stronghold was relentlessly firing from heavy machine guns. Apparently it was a suicide unit. It was firing at medical orderlies, wounded, women, and children crossing the street—in fact, all who came in sight. What was to be done?

For some time I had been hesitant to use the army's teams of flamethrower operators and had kept them in reserve. Now I made up my mind. I ordered a team with portable flamethrowers from the 41st Separate Engineers Brigade to be brought forward.

The flamethrower operators worked their way right up to the corner house and directed jets of burning liquid at all the firing ports and basement windows.

Infantry alone cannot do much against an enemy holed up in a building with thick brick walls. All types of weapons have to be used, particularly artillery, which has to provide continuous support. Experience shows that an assault group has to be supported by at least two or three artillery pieces in addition to the infantry's own heavy weapons.

The artillery would isolate an objective with interdiction fire, cutting it off from the flanks and rear, and denying its garrison all outside support. The guns also silence fire emplacements and prevent enemy counterattacks.

In street fighting, the longest range for artillery is between 300 and 400 yards, so gun crews have to act with the utmost precision and efficiency, open fire suddenly, and destroy their targets with the first or second shot to avoid their guns' being put out of action by the enemy.

It is often necessary to position a gun in a house and fire through a window. The gun crew cannot do this alone; the infantry helps to roll the heavy gun into place.

Reconnaissance, which preceded every attack, deserves special mention. Continuous reconnaissance operations provided information about the enemy's weak and strong points and consequently enabled the troops to act with every chance of success. Our scouts had to be brave and resourceful.

On April 27, the troops continued to storm old Berlin, capturing block after block. By dusk our main forces reached Tiergarten, the last defense line of the German forces in the city.

Attempts to cross the Landwehr Canal from march column failed. Tiergarten, an island surrounded by the waters of the Spree and the canals, was defended by handpicked SS troops and guard battalions, ensconced in tall, solid buildings, from which they kept all the approaches to the water barriers under observation and aimed fire.

We decided that the crossing of the canal should be made by small groups, not by entire regiments or divisions, and only in sectors where our guns had cleared the way and silenced every enemy weapon emplacement which could impede the operation. The choice of crossing points was left to the unit commanders. They were at the assault positions, with a better view of the results of the artillery fire, and could find the best spot to reach the objective with minimal losses.

While discussing preparations for storming Tiergarten, the Army Military Council also worked out measures to ensure the safety of German national treasures. Banks, book depositories, research centers, and medical institutions were to be protected by special teams from the logistical units. The Army Military Council undertook to ensure the safety of diplomatic missions, embassies, and consulates in Berlin.

We had also to take steps to provide food and medical services for the civilian population of Berlin. There were only a few tons of flour and a small supply of tinned fish and meat in Berlin's warehouses and food depots. There were no fresh meat, cereals, or dairy products. Berliners were starving. Children ran up to the Soviet tanks, even braving machine-gun and artillery fire, to get to our field kitchens.

Russian soldiers were feeding German children out of their mess kits. They gave them tinned food and sugar. Finally, field kitchens were specially deployed to feed Berliners.

Not more than 400 yards separated the Landwehr Canal from Voss Strasse and the Imperial Chancellery, in which Hitler had his last refuge and to which the troops of the 5th Shock Army were fighting their way. The approaches to it were manned by battalions of the Special SS Adolf Hitler Brigade under the command of the dyed-in-the-wool Nazi and Hitler's faithful servant, Mohnke.

Fifty minutes to zero hour. An ominous, tense silence, disturbed only by the crackling of burning buildings, hung over the city. Suddenly we heard a child crying. It seemed to come from somewhere underground. Muffled yet insistent, the child's voice kept repeating *"Mutter, mutter,"* a word all of us knew.

"Seems to be on the opposite bank," said Sergeant Masalov.

Machine guns began to stutter. Sergeant Masalov crawled forward, pressing himself to the ground, taking cover in shallow shell craters. He was careful to feel every bump and crack in the asphalt so as not to hit a mine. He got across the embankment and hid behind a projection of the concrete canal wall. He again heard the child's voice. It was calling pitifully and insistently, as if asking Masalov to hurry. Then Masalov stood up—a tall, strong soldier.

Masalov leaped over the parapet. A few more minutes passed. Enemy machine guns stopped firing for a moment. Holding their breath, our men waited for the child to cry out again. But no sound came. They waited five minutes, then ten more. Nothing. Had Masalov risked his life in vain? Some of the men began to get ready to charge. Then they heard Masalov's voice: "Attention! I have the child. Cover me! A machine gun on the right, on the balcony of the building with columns. Shut 'em up!"

But it was already time for the artillery preparation. General Pozharsky who commanded the army's artillery gave the order: "Ready. . . . Fire!"

Thousands of guns and mortars opened up on the enemy defenses, covering Masalov's withdrawal from the jaws of death with a three-year-old German girl in his arms.

The bombardment of Tiergarten lasted about an hour, steadily becoming more intensive. From my observation post I could see thick clouds of smoke and brick dust rising above the government blocks. The northerly wind blew one of these clouds to envelop my observation post, completely obscuring the already-dim disk of the sun. Twilight set in, and only rarely did I manage to catch a glimpse of the tall walls of the canal embankment on the opposite bank.

Judging by the sound of the explosions, our gunners were hammering their rather small number of targets with direct fire. Apparently they were firing along the streets, demolishing obstacles that blocked the approaches to the squares on the opposite bank. But enemy machine-gun emplacements hidden in side streets and behind street corners were impervious. They would open up as our infantrymen got there. I therefore told the unit commanders, "Don't be in a hurry! Send only small groups across the canal to start with, and only in sectors where the artillery has done its job."

Half an hour or so later, the unit commanders began to report that in many sectors designated for the crossing, the enemy was delivering intense flanking fire mainly from heavy machine guns and automatic antiaircraft guns.

My hunch had been right. "We are conducting reconnaissance in force. Continue detecting enemy weapon emplacements," I ordered. I wanted them to search for a way out and not throw the men straight into the deadly fire.

Evening set in. Our artillerymen specified their missions and began preparing for a fresh strike. Rifle battalions supported by tanks and engineers continued to clear the approaches to the canal and take up better positions.

Other armies also took time out to prepare for a decisive assault on Tiergarten. The 3rd Shock army brought in a whole fresh corps for attacking the Reichstag.

Skirmishes went on all through the night. Our units feigned activity to find out as much as they could about the enemy's fire system. In those sectors where our assault teams had come close to the canal, several crossings were simulated: the men threw sacks packed with wooden shavings and tied with belts into the water. The ruse worked: the enemy opened fire from all the machine guns and it remained for our men to flash-range them.

In the morning our artillerymen and mortar crews began to pound the enemy weapon emplacements detected earlier. Houses and other buildings in the bends of the canal were leveled to the ground. The assault teams began crossing the canal.

Since the tanks operating in the assault groups could

reach Tiergarten only across the bridges, our first job was to gain control of them. The heaviest fighting developed for what we called the Hunchbacked Bridge. In the teeth of enemy machine-gun fire, our sappers managed to remove the mines and defuse two powerful explosive bombs suspended under the girders of the bridge. The first attempt to cross the bridge failed. The tank is a big target, and as soon as one of them appeared in the square in front of the bridge, heavy fire rained down on it. A dug-in Tiger was shooting from somewhere far back inside Tiergarten.

One might have thought that the tank crews would give up their efforts to get their formidable machines across to Tiergarten. But once again it was the resourcefulness of the men that saved the situation. They hung smudge pots on a tank and ignited them when it approached the bridge. The sight of what apparently was a burning tank which roared on firing its gun threw the Germans into momentary confusion. These few seconds were enough for the tank to cross the bridge and hide in the yard of a corner house. Once there, the tankmen and the submachine gunners of the assault group began clearing the block, which we subsequently used as a springboard to develop our success.

After seizing several small bridgeheads on the opposite bank of the Landwehr Canal, the army began storming Tiergarten from the south. The spearheads of all the attacks, including those launched from the north, west, and east, converged on the center of the island where the Imperial Chancellery was located. Orders to continue the senseless resistance were still coming from there. Its underground bunkers became Hitler's last refuge. Prisoners said that he had not been seen since March. With him were Goebbels, Bormann, Chief of the General Staff Krebs, who had replaced Guderian, and many other high-ranking officials—about 600 people in all. This was the nerve center of troop control, and the termination of hostilities not only inside Berlin but throughout Germany depended largely on how soon Hitler's last citadel would fall.

North of the Imperial Chancellery, near the Brandenburg Gate, stood the Reichstag, a tall, domed building. It had been damaged by bombs and now was a huge shell, convenient to defend.

The Opera House, palaces, and museums all had been turned into powerful strongpoints.

Every step cost us lives and superhuman effort. The fighting for this last defense line of the Third Reich was marked by the mass heroism of the Soviet troops. The stone and brick rubble, the asphalt pavements of the squares and streets of the German capital were covered in their blood. They went into combat in the brilliant spring sunshine. They wanted to live. And it had been for the sake of life and happiness on earth that they plowed their way through fire and death from the banks of the Volga to Berlin.

In the evening of April 30 General Glazunov, Commander of the 4th Guards Rifle Corps, called. His voice animated with excitement, he reported, "A lieutenant-colonel of the German army has arrived at the forward position of the 102nd Guards Rifle Regiment with a white flag. He has a letter addressed to the Soviet Command. He asks to be taken immediately to our higher headquarters to convey an important message. He crosses the canal in the sector of the suspension bridge. He requests that we indicate the place and time for representatives of the German High Command to cross the line of the front."

"Tell him we are ready to receive emissaries. Let him lead them across in the sector where he has himself crossed the line, through the suspension bridge," I said.

We waited and waited in agonizing suspense. Only my aide and I were in the room. One hour and a half passed. It was the middle of the night, but we were wide awake.

Finally, at 3:55 A.M. on May 1, the door opened and a German general with an Iron Cross entered the room. This was General Krebs, Chief of the General Staff of the German Land Forces. He was accompanied by the Chief of Staff of the 56th Panzer Corps, General Staff Colonel von Dufwing, and an interpreter.

Without waiting for questions, Krebs said, "I'll speak of extremely secret matters. You are the first foreigner to be told that on April 30 Hitler departed out of this world of his own will; he has committed suicide."

Then Krebs read out Goebbels's letter to the Soviet Supreme Command in which negotiations were proposed.

Krebs handed me two other documents: the credentials authorizing him to conduct talks with the Soviet Supreme Command and Hitler's testament listing the members of the new Imperial Government and the High Command of the German Armed Forces.

I telephoned Marshal Zhukov and reported, "General Krebs, Chief of the General Staff of the German Land Forces, has come to me. He said that Hitler has committed suicide. Goebbels as chancellor and Bormann as chairman of the Nazi Party have authorized Krebs to negotiate an armistice. Krebs requests us to suspend combat operations so that the new government headed by Doenitz could meet and decide that question of the further course of war."

Zhukov said that he would report to Moscow at once and that I should stay on the line since there might be something requiring explanation.

After a minute or so, Marshal Zhukov spoke again. "Ask Krebs if they want to lay down arms and surrender or intend to talk peace."

I put the question to Krebs. He shrugged his shoulders. Then I told him that we could conduct talks only on Germany's full surrender to the Allies in the anti-Hitler coalition: the Soviet Union, the United States, and Britain. We were unanimous on this.

Krebs left. The emissary of the Third Reich had refused to accept surrender and did not want to stop the destruction of Berlin and needless loss on both sides, including German civilians.

The command was given to open maximum-intensity

fire and finish off the enemy as quickly as possible. Thousands of mortar and artillery shells rained on the enemy, especially in and around the Imperial Chancellery and the Reichstag.

This overwhelming and well-prepared artillery assault soon produced results. Messages and reports on successful actions of our troops began coming in.

By nightfall the battle began to peter out. The crackle of submachine-gun fire could still be heard in the street. Everyone needed sleep, but our nerves were so strained that sleep was impossible: the war was about to end.

It was 1:25 A.M. on May 2. Sporadic fighting still continued, and bursts of submachine-gun fire and explosions of hand grenades could be heard. I tried to get some rest and covered my head with a cavalry cloak. But the telephone rang again.

It was a report from the HQ of the 28th Corps. At 12:40 A.M. the 79th Guards Rifle Division had intercepted a radio message in Russian, which said: "Hello, hello! This is the 56th German Panzer Corps. We ask you to cease fire. At 12:50 our emissaries will be at the Potsdam Bridge. Identification: a white flag. Waiting for your reply."

I ordered a cease-fire immediately but only in the sector where the emissaries were to be met to inform HQ of the 56th Panzer Corps that the parliamentaries would be allowed to pass and would meet our officers at the place and time indicated.

The telephone rang again. This time the 47th Guards Rifle Division reported that our officers sent to the Potsdam Bridge had met the German emissaries, a colonel and two majors. Colonel von Dufwing, Chief of Staff of the 56th Panzer Corps, said they were authorized by Corps Commander General Weidling to inform the Soviet Command of his decision to stop resistance and surrender.

I issued orders that Colonel von Dufwing return to General Weidling and inform him that the surrender had been accepted. The two German majors were to remain with us.

At 6:00 A.M. on May 2, Commander of the 56th Panzer Corps General Weidling accompanied by two generals of his staff crossed the line and surrendered. Weidling declared that for the past six days he had also been in command of Berlin's defense.

I ordered German Glazunov to cease fire in the sector facing General Weidling's corps and to send the general to me.

Second-in-command of the front forces General Sokolovsky, who was with us, told Weidling, "Issue an order for complete surrender so that there will be no more pockets of resistance."

"We've run out of ammunition. Therefore the resistance can't last long."

Sokolovsky replied, "We know this. Issue an order for complete surrender and clear your conscience."

Weidling began drawing up a draft. All those present in the room spoke in an undertone.

Weidling handed me the paper without uttering a word. When we were reading it, we saw that the wording was not quite good. But of course he did not care about giving us a polished version.

At noon the Berlin garrison surrendered. We went out into the street. All was quiet. The silence—something we had all forgotten—had a ringing tone to it, or so it seemed.

The war was over. The long and arduous path had come to an end. If all the trenches in which I had been during the war and the routes of marches and turning maneuvers had been linked in a straight line, it would have circled the globe. And I am proud that I traversed this path, together with the officers and men of the 8th Army under enemy fire, crossing water barriers and mine fields.

15. In the Far East

Marshal of the Soviet Union Alexander Vasilevsky (1895–1977) served in the armed forces since 1915. During the Second World War he was a Deputy Chief of the General Staff, the Chief of the General Staff, and at the same time a Deputy Minister of Defense, coordinating the operations of a number of fronts. At the end of the war he commanded the Third Byelorussian Front. After the war he was the Chief of the General Staff, a Deputy Minister, and the Minister of Defense, and the Inspector General of the USSR Ministry of Defense.

During the Soviet Union's war against Japan he was appointed Commander-in-Chief of the Soviet troops in the Far East.

I first heard that I should have to go to the Far East in the summer of 1944. After the Byelorussian operation, Stalin told me that I would be given command of troops in the Far East in the war with militarist Japan. I had already had an inkling of such a war when the Soviet delegation headed by Stalin had returned from the Teheran Conference. I had then been told that the Soviet delegation had given the Allies agreement in principle to help in the war against Japan.

The Soviet Union, however, had its own vital interests for joining the war with Japan. For many years the Japanese militarists had harbored plans of seizing the Soviet Far East. They had almost constantly perpetrated acts of military provocation on Soviet borders. They were holding large military forces ready to attack the Soviet Union in their strategic bridgeheads in Manchuria.

The situation grew particularly menacing when Nazi Germany had launched its vicious war against the Soviet Union. To combat the aggressor, we needed every fresh division we could lay our hands on, but we still kept several armies in full battle readiness in the Far East. Japan was just awaiting a suitable moment to start a war against the Soviet Union.

As soon as the East Prussian operation was over, I was summoned to the GHQ from the Third Byelorussian Front to take up duties as Deputy People's Defense Commissar. At that time the general staff was fully occupied with the Far Eastern theater of war.

We took into consideration the fact that the Kwantung Army had doubled its forces over the summer of 1945. The Japanese command maintained two-thirds of its tanks, half its artillery, and the crack imperial divisions in Manchuria and Korea. The Kwantung Army was commanded by the experienced Japanese General of the Army Yamada and his chief of staff, Lieutenant-General Hata, who had previously been military attaché in the Soviet Union. The Japanese army in the Far East together with the troops of the local puppets totaled over 1,200,000 men. It embraced three fronts: the First East Manchurian Front, stretching along our Maritime borders (ten infantry divisions and one infantry brigade in all); the Third West Manchurian Front designated for action on the Mongolian-Manchurian border (nine infantry divisions, three infantry, and two tank brigades in all); the 17th Front (Korean), located in Korea and operationally subordinated to the Kwantung Army commander (nine infantry divisions and five infantry brigades in all); the 4th Separate Army (three infantry divisions and four infantry brigades), designated for action on the northeastern borders of Manchuria. Units of the Fifth Front (three infantry divisions, one infantry brigade, a separate tank regiment) and a separate infantry regiment were deployed in southern Sakhalin and the Kurile Islands. The 2nd Air Force covered Manchuria from the air, while the 5th Air Force covered Korea.

The Japanese command had at its disposal in Manchuria the armies of Manchukuo, Inner Mongolia, and the Suiyuan Army Group which totaled 8 infantry and 7 cavalry divisions, 14 infantry and cavalry brigades.

The Japanese militarists had established in Manchuria along the borders with the Soviet Union and the Mongolian People's Republic as many as 17 fortified areas. Each fortified area was up to 30 miles in depth and between 30 and 60 miles in breadth along the front. Their purpose was not only to bolster defense, but also to create more favorable conditions for concentrating and deploying troops. The frontier fortified areas consisted of three lines.

The plan of campaign in the Far East which we had drawn up in the general staff was approved by GHQ. The plan envisaged launching the main attack from the Transbaikal area and the territory of the Mongolian People's Republic in the direction of Changchun (Xinzang), and Shenyang (Mukden). Its objective was to bring up the main groupings of Soviet troops from the south and cut the Third Front of the Kwantung Army in two.

The oncoming strong attack was planned from the Maritime region, out of the area to the south of Lake Hanka in the direction of Chilin (Kirin), by troops of the First Far Eastern Front. After linking up at this point, troops of this and the Transbaikal fronts were to press in the direction of Mukden and Port Arthur, which ensured the complete encirclement of the main forces of the Kwantung Army in the shortest possible time.

In taking this decision, GHQ and the general staff knew that both Far Eastern fronts did not have sufficient forces for defeating the Japanese troops and bringing the war to a rapid end. Therefore we carried out an urgent regrouping of our forces and supplies from the western theater of war to the Far East.

The three field and one tank armies being moved from the west to the Far East alone had a total of 12 corps, or 39 divisions and brigades. In addition, we transferred several other formations and units of all branches of the forces and types of service.

But this was not a simple quantitative increase in troops. A regrouping of units and large formations that best suited the specific conditions of the Far Eastern theater of war was carried out. Their place in the operational structure of fronts in the Far East depended on their experience and quality. Thus the 5th and 39th armies with their command personnel were shifted from Eastern Prussia because they were proficient at piercing defensive zones.

The 6th Guards Tank and the 53rd Field armies brought up from Prague to the Transbaikal Front were to advance through the mountains and steppes, fighting over wide expanses and in separate lines of advance.

Implementation of the regrouping operations was fraught with enormous difficulties. It too place in conditions of strict camouflage. Some 136,000 railway carriages with troops and supplies arrived in the Far East and the Transbaikal area in four months (May–August) alone.

All in all, by August 1945, the Supreme Command of the Soviet troops in the Far East had deployed eleven field armies, two task forces, one tank army, three air armies, three air defense armies, and four separate air corps. Further, it had the support of the Pacific Fleet (including the Northern Pacific Flotilla) and the Amur Naval Flotilla. The frontier detachments would also be used.

All the troops concentrated in the Far East by order of

GHQ were combined into three fronts: the Transbaikal, the First, and the Second Far Eastern fronts.

The Transbaikal Front under the command of Marshal Malinovsky consisted of the 17th, 36th, 39th, and 53rd Field armies, the 6th Guards Tank, and the 12th Air Force armies, an air defense army, and a cavalry and mechanized group of the Soviet-Mongolian troops.

The First Far Eastern Front under the command of Marshal Meretskov included the 1st, 5th, 25th, and 35th Field armies, the Chuguyevka Task Force, the 10th Mechanized Corps, the 9th Air Army, and an air defense army.

The Second Far Eastern Front under the command of General Purkayev included the 2nd, 15th, and 16th Field armies, the 5th Separate Rifle Corps, the Kamchatka Defensive Area, the 10th Air Army, and an air defense army.

In order to be able to command the front efficiently and uninterruptedly in such conditions, the High Command of Soviet troops in the Far East and its HQ were set up. As had been decided beforehand, I was appointed the Commander-in-Chief, Colonel-General Shilin, a member of the Military Council, and Colonel-General Ivanov, the Chief of Staff.

I arrived by special train at Chita on July 5 with documents in the name of Colonel-General Vasilyev. For the sake of secrecy, I was also dressed in a colonel-general's uniform.

I should make the point that my provisional army rank occasionally embarrassed officers who had known me earlier. When I would arrive in a unit or formation, the duty officer would approach to make a report, as instructed, to Colonel-General Vasilyev, and he would be surprised to see Vasilevsky in the uniform of a colonel-general.

First I got to know the troops of the Transbaikal Front. Together with Malinovsky, I went round all the major sectors. We did some reconnoitering and discussed the situation and the coming battle assignments with the commanding officers of armies, corps, and the main divisions.

On July 16 I received a telephone call from Stalin in Potsdam while I was at the HQ of the Far Eastern troops located 15 miles southwest of Chita. It was on the eve of the opening of the Potsdam Three-Power Conference. He asked how preparations were going on and whether the operation could be brought forward by something like ten days. I reported that the concentration of troops and the transportation of supplies would not permit that, and I asked him to stick to the previous date. Stalin gave his consent. Why Stalin had asked me this question on the eve of the conference he did not tell me. Sometime later I learned that, according to American plans to defeat Japan which had been worked out before the Potsdam Conference and approved by the U.S. President on June 29, the landing of American troops on the island of Kyushu was to take place on November 1, 1945, with a landing on the island of Honshu not earlier than March 1, 1946.

We received a GHQ directive on August 7 ordering the troops of the Transbaikal, First, and Second Far East fronts to commence hostilities on August 9.

On the night of August 8, the forward battalions and scout detachments of the three fronts advanced into enemy territory in extremely foul weather conditions: a summer monsoon bringing frequent and heavy downpours. At dawn the main forces of the Transbaikal and First Far Eastern fronts launched their offensive and crossed the state border of the Soviet Union. At that time I was in the area of the First Far Eastern Front HQ which had moved before hostilities started from around Voroshilovsk to the taiga (swampy forest) into specially constructed houses. The High Command HQ remained near Chita.

Our joint advance with the Mongolian People's Revolutionary Army developed successfully from the very first hours of the war. The surprise and strength of the initial attacks enabled Soviet troops immediately to take the initiative. The beginning of the military operation by the Soviet Union caused panic in the Japanese government. Prime Minister Suzuki announced on August 9 that ''the entry this morning of the Soviet Union into the war puts us once and for all in a helpless position and makes the continuance of the war impossible.'' Thus, it was precisely the actions of the Soviet armed forces, on the admission of the Japanese leadership, and not the atomic bombing of the Japanese cities by American planes on August 6 and 9 that decided Japan's fate and accelerated the ending of the Second World War.

The mass annihilation of the inhabitants of Japanese cities was not dictated by any military need. The atom bomb was, in the eyes of the U.S. leaders, not so much the final act in the Second World War as the first act in the cold war against the Soviet Union.

The advance of Soviet troops encountered fierce resistance. Nonetheless, Soviet troops performed their missions splendidly in all the main lines of advance. Already by August 11 the forward units of the Transbaikal Front had reached the western slopes of the Great Hingan, while the mobile troops of the main grouping had crossed it and reached the Central Manchurian Plain. The crossing of the Khingan Range was a feat unprecedented in modern warfare. By the end of August 14, troops of the Transbaikal Front had covered a distance of between 150 and 250 miles, reached the central regions of Manchuria, and were continuing to advance toward its capital, Changchun, and the big industrial center of Mukden. During all this time, troops of the First Far Eastern Front, which had had to cope with the almost impassable mountainous and swampy terrain, had broken through strong lines of defense, advanced into Manchuria to a depth of 75 to 95 miles, and engaged in battle for the town of Mutankiang. Troops of the Second Far Eastern Front were fighting on the approaches to Tsitsihar and Kiamusze. Thus, by the end of six days of the Soviet offensive, the Kwantung Army had been split into several sections.

Faced by inevitable military defeat, the Japanese government decided to capitulate on August 14. The next day, Premier Suzuki's cabinet fell. However, troops of the Kwantung Army continued their stubborn resistance.

In the next few days, the Soviet troops engaged in the offensive picked up speed rapidly. Over a 625-mile sector of the Transbaikal Front, a cavalry and mechanized group reached Kalgan and Chengteh (Jehol). The 17th Army was advancing to the shores of the Bay of Liaotun. The 6th Guards Tank Army, which was experiencing considerable difficulties with supplies, was nevertheless resolving the main mission of the front to take Mukden. The 39th Army had repaired bridges and railway lines destroyed by the retreating enemy and was advancing through Taoan toward Changchun.

Then the 53rd Army was brought into action from the second wave into the breach that had formed between the 17th and 39th armies. It advanced on Fuxing through Kaila. As a result, troops of the Transbaikal Front had reached the areas of Chifeng, Changchun, Mukden, Kaitung and Tsitsihar by August 19. This meant that an enormous wedge had been thrust into the Kwantung Army from the west by the Soviet armed forces over an area of approximately 235,000 square miles.

Troops of the First Far Eastern Front also continued their advance. On August 16, the 35th Army reached and took the Kiamusze-Tumyin railway line and thereby firmly secured the right flank of the main front grouping, cutting off the Japanese 4th Separate Army, pushed by troops of the Second Far Eastern Front to the south, from the Mutankiang grouping. At that time the 1st and 5th armies were engaged in heavy fighting for the major railway and road junctions and the important administrative and political center of Mutankiang. Putting up a spirited defense and counterattacking frequently, the enemy finally surrendered the town on August 16. In this fighting the Kwantung Army lost more than 40,000 officers and men. Together with the 19th Mechanized Corps, the 25th Army captured the town of Wangquing which covered the approaches to Chilin and the northern regions of Korea on the same day. Simultaneously, its troops linked up with a marine landing force and took the major naval base of Seisin and reached the communications line of the Japanese 3rd Army, cutting of the troops of the 17th Front from the First Front and from the coast of the Sea of Japan.

By the end of the first week of the war, the Japanese 5th Army had been routed and the 3rd Army and other troops of the First Front had suffered heavy casualties. The enemy's attempt to stop at all costs the advance of Soviet troops into the Central Manchurian Plain and toward North Korea had come to grief.

Operations to liberate Korea also went ahead successfully, as part of the campaign of Soviet troops in the Far East. The 25th Army carried out the main mission in cooperation with the Pacific Fleet. On August 12 they captured the North Korean towns of Yuki and Racine (Najin). With the arrival of Soviet troops at Seisin (Chongjin), the Kwantung Army defenses in the maritime area were fully smashed. Sea and air landings were also made in several ports and towns of North Korea. In early September, Soviet troops reached the 38th parallel set up by agreement of the Allied Powers.

Meanwhile, troops of the Second Far Eastern Front captured the town of Kiamusze and, jointly with the Amur Naval Flotilla, advanced along the Sungari to Harbin. The Soviet Air Force dominated the skies in the whole theater of war. The Pacific Fleet firmly secured the coasts of North Korea. The Kwantung Army suffered a crushing defeat.

At 5:00 P.M. on August 17, a wireless message was received from Commander-in-Chief of the Kwantung Army General Yamada telling us that he had issued an order to the Japanese troops to halt hostilities at once and to lay down their arms to Soviet troops. At 7:00 P.M. a Japanese plane dropped two message bags in the sector of the First Far Eastern Front informing us, in the name of the staff of the First Front of the Kwantung Army, that they were halting the fighting. However, in most of the sectors, the Japanese troops continued not only to put up resistance, but in some places to launch counterattacks.

I ordered the commander of the First Far Eastern Front to send staff officers to airfields at Mutankiang and Muling with powers to inform Kwantung Army staff representatives that Soviet troops would halt their action only when the Japanese troops began to surrender. This measure had to be taken because many Japanese army units and garrisons either had not received Yamada's order through loss of contact or had refused to carry it out. On August 18, at 3:00 A.M. Yamada replied by radio to the Soviet Supreme Command, stating his readiness to fulfill all the terms of the capitulation. Japanese units started to surrender in many sectors of the front on August 18.

To speed up the disarmament of the capitulating Japanese troops and the liberation of territories they had captured, I issued the following order on August 18, to troops of the Transbaikal, First, and Second Far Eastern fronts:

Owing to the fact that Japanese resistance has been crushed and the poor state of the roads badly hampers the swift movement of our main troops in performing their missions, we need to switch to action by specially formed, highly mobile and well-equipped detachments in order to capture the towns of Changchun, Mukden, Chilin, and Harbin immediately. These and similar detachments can be also used for dealing with subsequent assignments without fear of their being too far away from their main forces.

These detachments had been formed in all armies out of tank units, infantry units in motor vehicles, and units of the self-propelled and antitank artillery. Air landings had been made in Mukden, Changchun, Port Arthur, Dalny,

Harbin, and Chilin to capture the main military and industrial facilities and to accept the capitulation of their garrisons. Following the air landings, forward detachments and then units and formations of the 6th Guards Tanks Army entered Mukden, Changchun, Port Arthur, and Dalny.

On August 18, an air landing force in Harbin unexpectedly came upon Chief of Staff of the Kwantung Army, Lieutenant-General Hata, at the airfield. It was suggested that he fly by Soviet plane to the command post of the commander of the First Far Eastern Front to coordinate questions related to the capitulation of the Kwantung Army. Hata accepted this proposal and at 3:30 P.M. (Far Eastern time) on August 19 a meeting took place with him and the Japanese consul in Harbin, Miyakawa.

We set forth demands on the capitulation procedure, indicated the assembly points for prisoners of war, the movement routes, and the time. Hata accepted all the terms. He explained the disregard of the surrender order by a few Japanese units and formations due to the delay in the Kwantung Army's transmitting the capitulation order to them, since the Kwantung Army staff had lost control of its troops on the second day of the Red Army offensive. Further, we warned Hata that Japanese troops had to surrender in an organized way, together with their officers, and that, in the first few days of the capitulation, the feeding of their troops would be the concern of the Japanese leadership. The troops would have to surrender with their kitchen trains; the Japanese generals were to appear with their adjutants and their personal effects. It was also announced that we would guarantee decent treatment both of high-ranking officers and of all servicemen.

From August 19 onward, Japanese troops began to capitulate almost everywhere. As many as 148 Japanese generals and 594,000 officers and men were taken prisoner. By the end of August, the Kwantung Army and other enemy forces stationed in Manchuria and North Korea were completely disarmed. The operations to liberate south-

ern Sakhalin and the Kurile Islands had been crowned with
success.

The campaign by the Soviet armed forces in the Far
East had ended in a brilliant victory. It is impossible to
overestimate its importance. Officially, the campaign lasted
24 days. The enemy's main striking forces had been utterly defeated. The Japanese militarists had been deprived
of bridgeheads for aggression, and their major supply bases
for raw materials and arms in China, Korea, and in southern Sakhalin. The rout of the Kwantung Army accelerated
the capitulation of Japan as a whole.

The ending of the war in the Far East saved hundreds of
thousands of American and British soldiers from death,
millions of Japanese citizens from incalculable casualties
and suffering, and averted the further slaughter and plun-
der of the peoples of East and Southeast Asia by Japanese
occupying forces.

Index